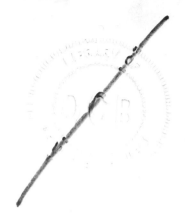

The WATCHTOWER HERESY
versus THE BIBLE

By

TED DENCHER

MOODY PRESS

ORDER FROM
OSTERHUS BOOK & BIBLE HOUSE
4500 WEST BROADWAY
MINNEAPOLIS, MIN'N, 55422

Printed in the United States of America

CONTENTS

THE APOSTLE'S CREED

I BELIEVE in God the Father Almighty, Maker of heaven and earth; and in Jesus Christ His only Son our Lord; who was conceived by the Holy Ghost, born of the Virgin Mary, suffered under Pontius Pilate, was crucified, dead and buried; He descended into hell; the third day He rose again from the dead; He ascended into heaven, and sitteth at the right hand of God the Father Almighty; from thence He shall come to judge the quick and the dead. I believe in the Holy Ghost; the holy catholic church; the communion of saints; the forgiveness of sins; the resurrection of the body and the life everlasting. Amen.

NOTE:

All quotations from the Bible are taken from the *American Standard Version* unless otherwise stated.

FOREWORD

THIS BOOK would never have been possible aside from the saving power of the Lord Jesus Christ. Having come into the error of the Watchtower Society in 1946, it wasn't until 1957 that deliverance came; it really began back in 1953.

It was then that I was invited to present Watchtower beliefs against that of the Gospel of Christ. A series of meetings were held, totaling many hours of discussion. One Biblical fact was impressed upon my mind: THE BIBLE SEEMED TO TEACH THAT JESUS CHRIST IS GOD! Naturally, my entire being rebelled against the thought. But I believed it had to be proved or disproved one way or the other.

A searching of Scripture for over three years began. This involved the Greek text of the New Testament. The evidence was overwhelming! Every text bearing upon the subject stated that Jesus Christ is Almighty God! Not only that, but it seemed to me that what He accomplished upon Calvary somehow atoned for our sins.

Now began a searching of conscience. The Watchtower Society refused to answer eight questions submitted to them regarding *The New World Translation of the Christian Greek Scriptures*. I was convinced after receiving no answer that their translation is a fraud. I could see the conflict between the Watchtower and the Bible. I had to choose one and reject the other. Which would it be?

God helped me decide. One night I was caused to behold a mental scene so vivid it was almost real. I gazed up at the sky and could picture Calvary. The whole sky seemed to hold the Cross. Christ hung on that Cross for me! In the horror and awe of the moment I knew it was true—He *had* died for me! So personal was His love that if I were the only sinner ever born on this earth, He would have left the mansions of

5

glory, come to this sin-cursed earth, to atone for *my* sins. So then I knew that He was my *personal* Saviour. It was *His* person given for *my* person—substitutionary atonement. From that moment of belief, I count my new life in Christ.

One of the men who had dealt with me in 1953 then wrote me. In my answer I told what had happened to me. Then he wanted to know what I thought of Christ. Was He man, angel, or God? I was not sure about anything else, but this one thing I knew: Jesus was God and He had died for me. God had saved this sinner's soul.

Chapter One

THE HOLY SPIRIT—*HE* OR *IT?*

JEHOVAH'S WITNESSES are led to believe that the Holy Spirit is merely a force in action, not the third Person of the Trinity. Who leads them to think thus? Their organizational mind, the Watchtower Society, the world headquarters of which is in New York City. Let us read some of the statements made in their publications. These statements are parroted earth-wide by the Witnesses, for they witness to what THE WATCHTOWER SOCIETY says and does, thus making them in reality WATCHTOWER WITNESSES!

Quoting from the magazine *Consolation* (now called *Awake!*) of January 7, 1942, we read the following from the pen of "Judge" Rutherford, who was then president of the Watchtower Society: "The religious clergy teach that the so-called 'holy ghost' is the third person of what they call 'the triune god.' " ... "The *holy spirit* (mistranslated *holy ghost*) is not a person or being, and no scripture authorizes such a conclusion." Needless to say, he quotes no Scripture to support this, his *own* conclusions but makes statements which the Witnesses accept without question.

"Judge" Rutherford was only repeating what the founder of the Society, Charles Taze Russell taught regarding the Holy Spirit. Mere statements from the Society satisfy the Witnesses; they do not require that the Bible confirm them. Without Biblical authority for their beliefs, they live in hope that someday the Society will provide a basis for them. "Judge" Rutherford was notorious for his negative attitude toward all clergymen and all government. It was this man who helped form the Society into what it is today!

Quoting now from *The Watchtower* magazine (the *logos* of the Watchtower Society) of August 15, 1944, we read under the caption *Comforter, Paraclete:* "The spirit or helper

7

is not a spirit person or personage, but is the ACTIVE FORCE of God . . ." (emphasis mine). The strange part of this article is that further on it quotes Acts 5:3 which reads: "Satan has filled thy heart to deceive the Holy Spirit." It is strange, because YOU CANNOT DECEIVE A MERE FORCE! Of course, the Society hopes that under the weight of Watchtower writings this problem will be overlooked. They try to "drown" the Scriptures in Watchtower material. If it were otherwise, the Witnesses would soon begin to realize that the Watchtower and the Bible are at odds. Then there would be some embarrassing problems for the Watchtower Society to face.

The book *New Heavens And A New Earth* in discussing the operation of the Spirit in creation, as recorded in Genesis 1:2 (page 38) states: "It was not the supposed third person of an imaginary, unscriptural 'trinity.'" But, in *The Watchtower* magazine of April 15, 1958, page 236, there is a picture that supposedly shows the Son of God pouring out the Holy Spirit upon the disciples at Pentecost!

In this article the Spirit is depicted by lines representing energy, coming from Christ to the disciples. Thus they show what they believe the Holy Spirit to be. It also confuses the issue as to their belief regarding Jesus Christ. They believe that He was resurrected as a spirit, not in the physical body. Yet they picture Him in Heaven with a physical body! We shall deal with this subject at length in the next chapter.

Actually, the Watchtower denies the EXISTENCE of the Holy Spirit, i.e., conscious, personal existence. Therefore, He "exists" only in the sense that an object without life "exists." We do not believe that a chair, for example, possesses equal existence with us. We quote the *Funk and Wagnalls Standard Home Reference Dictionary* on the word *exist:* "Have actual being . . . to continue animate or in the exercise of vital functions; live; as animal life cannot *exist* without oxygen. Being, or the state or fact of being or continuing to be, whether as substance, essence, personality or consciousness . . . Possession or continuance of animate or vital being; life; as, a fight for *existence.*"

The Watchtower denies a high level of existence for the Holy Spirit. We humans need oxygen in order to exist. Does the oxygen also exist? If so, what does *it* need in order to exist? Actually, oxygen does not exist as we do. Does God exist? Not as we do! He is above our form of existence. The Watchtower, in putting the Holy Spirit on a level with energy, *denies* His existence even on our own level, putting Him below the level of humanity!

The Watchtower insists that their idea of the Holy Spirit is the *only one* a Witness may accept. *The Watchtower* magazine of November 1, 1954 states: "The holy spirit MUST be recognized as THE ACTIVE FORCE of Jehovah. . . ." (Emphasis mine). They have stated their position clearly and cannot deny it now. It falls upon us, therefore, to expose their heresy thoroughly and completely. To that end we will examine the Greek text of which the English New Testament is a translation, in order to demonstrate the errors of the Watchtower Society.

We now go to their favorite book, called *Let God Be True.* Under the caption, *The Holy Spirit,* it is argued that the Holy Spirit is not a person: "A little searching of any Greek-English dictionary will reveal that the Greek word *pneuma* translated 'spirit' is the same word translated also in the Bible as 'wind.' " This is a deceptive kind of reasoning. Although the Greek dictionary does give the above definition, of the 385 times the Greek word *pneuma* occurs in *The Watchtower* translation, only once is it translated "wind" (John 3:8). In other passages it would not make sense to translate *pneuma* as "wind." For example: "I will pray the Father, and he shall give you another Comforter, that he may be with you forever, even the 'wind' of truth; whom the world cannot receive; for it beholdeth him not, neither knoweth him; for he abideth with you and shall be in you" (John 14:16-17). It is not reasonable to draw a conclusion from one difficult passage when 384 other passages using the same Greek word indicate a different translation.

Well, if PNEUMA does not mean *wind,* what word does?

The Greek word ANEMOS. It occurs 31 times and is rendered 31 times as *wind,* and it never means *Spirit!* Now if God, who inspired the Scriptures to be written (II Timothy 3:16) wanted the word PNEUMA to mean *wind,* He would NOT have had the writers use the word ANEMOS. Or did God make a mistake? If the word PNEUMA means *wind,* then ANEMOS must (to the same extent) mean *Spirit!* If so, then the words would be interchangeable. No, ANEMOS does not mean *Spirit,* and PNEUMA does not mean *wind.* Therefore the statement in the *Let God Be True* book is a LIE!

In the New Testament the Holy Spirit carries the masculine gender *He.* Does this denote that the Holy Spirit is mere energy or force? Or, is the Holy Spirit a person? The Greek word EKEINOS gives the Holy Spirit masculine gender at John 14:26; 15:26; 16:8, 13-15; etc. The inspired writer had THREE WORDS that he could have used: EKEINE, feminine gender; EKEINO, neuter gender, and EKEINOS, masculine gender. God chose for the writer to use the MASCULINE GENDER EKEINOS. Did God make a mistake in referring to the Holy Spirit as a person?

At John 14:26 we read: "He shall TEACH YOU ALL THINGS." A force could not teach *anything,* much less ALL things! This suggests conscious personality. At John 14:16 the Holy Spirit is called COMFORTER. This suggests His comforting us with His person, hence, personal comfort. See also John 16:13, where the Greek expression EKEINOS TO PNEUMA TES ALETHEIA, HE THE SPIRIT OF TRUTH occurs, again showing the Holy Spirit to be a person. Verse 14 also uses EKEINOS—"*He* will glorify me." The fact that a person is glorifying suggests a *personal* glory; a force could not glorify of its own initiative. In Matthew 12:32-33 we read: "Every sin and blasphemy shall be forgiven unto men; but the BLASPHEMY AGAINST THE SPIRIT shall not be forgiven . . . Whosoever shall speak against THE HOLY SPIRIT, it shall not be forgiven him, neither in this world, nor in that which is to come."

Does it seem reasonable that one should be condemned for speaking against a mere force or an energy? No wonder the Watchtower remains silent on this subject. In order to blaspheme a personality there must of necessity be a person. And it follows that in order to blaspheme the Holy Spirit *personally,* the Holy Spirit must be a person. You cannot blaspheme a person unless that person exists.

There are two significant points we might well consider now. This involves the Trinity as a whole. One is the baptism of Jesus, when the Holy Spirit descended as a dove. You might compare this with Genesis 1:2 where the Spirit was "brooding upon the face of the waters" (as a bird broods over her young). This indicates conscious, personal life. Also, we are to be baptized in the name (singular) of "the Father and of the Son and of the Holy Spirit." Thus each has a personal name. The Holy Spirit is not classified separately as a thing.

After Ananias had lied to the Holy Spirit as recorded at Acts 5:3, he was told that he had lied to God (Acts 5:4). If God is a person then so is the Holy Spirit. Acts 28:25 reads: "Well SPAKE the Holy Spirit through Isaiah the prophet unto your fathers." Then follows a quote from Isaiah 6:9, 10. The verse preceding this quote reads: "And I heard the voice of the Lord, saying, Whom shall *I* send, and who will go for *us?*" (Isaiah 6:8). How could He speak if He were not a person? Once again we see the deity and personality of the Holy Spirit in the teaching of the Trinity in the Scriptures.

At Psalm 139:7 the Spirit is OMNIPRESENT, and at I Corinthians 2:10 He is OMNISCIENT, both indicating personality. At Romans 8:27 we read of the "MIND of the Spirit." How could a force or an energy have a mind of its own?

The Watchtower has found that these embarrassing texts are better ignored! Having no answer they remain silent. The Witnesses, left on their own, will make a feeble effort by saying that there is no neuter gender in the Greek; but in saying this they show ignorance of the language concerning which they represent themselves as students and scholars. They are neither. They have been grossly deceived, and in turn are deceiving others.

Regarding the baptism of the Holy Spirit, the book *New*

Heavens And A New Earth, page 306, reads: "Peter told the listening multitude that if they believed the message, repented and were baptized in water and in the name of Jesus Christ, they too would be baptized with the holy spirit, receiving it as a free gift."

Now here is what the *Bible* says: "While Peter yet spake these words, the Holy Spirit fell on all them that heard the word. And they of the circumcision that believed were amazed, as many as came with Peter, because that on the Gentiles also was poured out the gift of the Holy Spirit. For they heard them speak with tongues, and magnify God. Then answered Peter, Can any man forbid the water, that these should not be baptized, who have received the Holy Spirit as well as we? And he commanded them to be baptized in the name of Jesus Christ." (Taken from Acts 10:44-48.)

In the above account we find the opposite to what the Watchtower says. They received the baptism of the Holy Spirit *first,* then the water baptism. In Acts 11:5-17 Peter relates the account of how he was led to bring about the conversion of certain Gentiles, who received the baptism of the Holy Spirit at their conversion, not after a water baptism.

The book *New Heavens And A New Earth* continues, page 306: "A believer may be baptized in water in symbol of his unconditional dedication to Jehovah God, yet if he does not get the baptism with the holy spirit from God through Christ, he will never enter the kingdom of the heavens to reign with Christ." Only the 144,000 are supposed to enter the heavens according to the Witnesses. All Jehovah's Witnesses who believe themselves to be outside this number will freely admit they are strangers to the indwelling, baptizing Holy Spirit. Romans 8:9 clearly tells us: "But ye are not in the flesh but in the Spirit, if so be that the Spirit of God dwelleth in you. But if any man hath not the Spirit of Christ, he is none of his."

Note carefully the following quoted from *The Holy Spirit* by John Owen:

He who knows no more of the ministry of the gospel than what consists in an attention to the letter of institutions, and the manner of their performance, knows nothing of it. Not that there is any extraordinary inspiration now pretended to by us, as some slanderously report, but there is that presence of the Spirit of God with the ministry of the gospel, in his authority, assistance, communication of gifts and abilities, guidance and direction, without which it is useless and unprofitable. . . .

There is a spiritual leprosy spread over our nature, which renders us loathsome to God, and puts us in a state of separation from him, as those of old, who were legally unclean, were separated from the congregation, and from all the pledges of God's gracious presence—Numbers 5:2. Whatever men do of themselves, to be rid of this defilement, only hides but cannot remove it. Adam cured neither his nakedness nor the shame of it, by his fig leaves . . . Whatever we do of ourselves is a covering, not a cleansing.

And if we die in this condition, unwashed, uncleansed, unpurified, it is impossible that ever we should be admitted into the blessed presence of the holy God—Revelation 21:27. Let no man deceive you with vain words. It is not doing a few good works, it is not an outward profession of religion, that will give you "access with boldness" to God.

Shame will cover you when it will be too late. Unless you are washed by the Spirit of God, and in the blood of Christ, you shall not inherit the kingdom of God . . . If therefore you would not perish as base defiled creatures, when your pride . . . and your duties will stand you in no stead—look out betimes for that only way of purification which God has ordained. But if you love your defilements, if you are proud of your pollutions, if you satisfy yourselves with your outward ornaments—there is no remedy, you must perish forever.

Further on in his book John Owen remarks:

If the Holy Ghost were only a power or force, then sin against God would automatically be sin against the

Holy Spirit also. But—the Spirit can be sinned against separate from the Father—apart from the Father! The Holy Ghost may be distinctly blasphemed, or be the immediate object of that sin, which is inexpiable. To suppose, therefore, that this Holy Ghost is not a Divine Person is for men to dream while they seem to be awake.

The Witnesses would probably believe what the Bible teaches if it were not for the WATCHTOWER PUBLICATIONS which keep them from it! Under the guise of Biblical instruction these publications lead the reader AWAY FROM THE BIBLE, gradually, until the Bible is used only, in its misinterpretation, to support the Watchtower publications!

Jehovah's Witnesses (misnamed people who are really WATCHTOWER WITNESSES) study in neighborhood groups as BOOK STUDIES. They have neither BIBLE studies nor prayer meetings. They have neither worship services nor devotions. They sing neither hymns nor praise to God or Christ—only to the organization.

In their lives there is neither grace nor salvation. No joy in the Lord, no comfort of the Spirit; no freedom of the sons of God! Only there is a constant drudgery of arguing and debating from door-to-door, making out reports to headquarters on what they have or have not done for the organization. Such is the sad, pitiful state of those who have denied the personality of Holy Spirit.

How far, yes, how *very* far they have strayed from the Christian faith! Yet they claim that theirs is the only true faith, and all others are of the Devil! To them every denomination, except their own, is of the Devil. All their friends and relatives, if they are not Jehovah's Witnesses, are the Devil's people. They believe that the church was in darkness from the times of the apostles until 1872, when Charles Taze Russell came upon the scene.

All the great men of God from the first century to the twentieth century are scorned by the Witnesses. In John Owen's book mention is made of those church fathers "that those who scorn these things may reflect on whose ashes they trample."

But our subject is far from complete. The Witness will now demand further proof on the subject of the Trinity. "Was not Jesus only a man?" he will ask. "Do we not ignore many Scriptures in our efforts to create a Trinity? How could there be a Trinity seeing that Jesus was inferior to His Father? Was He not created by this very Father?" These questions we leave for the following two chapters to answer. For we will now begin a study of the deity of the Lord Jesus Christ, which will then lead us on into bringing the three persons together, concluding with the chapter on the Trinity.

Chapter Two

THE DEITY OF JESUS CHRIST

THE WATCHTOWER desires that Jesus Christ be a creature. (Few realize that the Watchtower teaches that Michael the archangel became Messiah, who had to obtain the new birth as does any sinner!) The Deity of Jesus Christ, however, is taught throughout the entire Bible. A volume could be written on this subject alone! Let us begin our investigation with the promise of Messiah to come, as found in the Old Testament.

In the book of Genesis we find an equality between the divine Persons of the Godhead. Genesis 1:26, 27: "And God said, Let US make man in OUR image, after OUR likeness . . . And God created man in HIS own image, in the image of God created HE them." This is similar to the language found at Genesis 11:7, 8 concerning the time of the Tower of Babel: "Come, let US go down, and there confound their language, that they may not understand one another's speech. So JEHOVAH scattered them abroad . . . ."

At Isaiah 9:6 a prophecy is found referring to Messiah as "the mighty God." Quoting *The Holy Scriptures According to the Masoretic Text,* this verse is number five in chapter nine: "And his name is called Wonderful in counsel is God the Mighty, the everlasting Father, the Ruler of peace." Jehovah's Witnesses will be quick to point out that he is called *mighty, not* ALMIGHTY. So we will be quick to point out in return that so is Jehovah! Where? At Isaiah 10:21 and Jeremiah 32:18! In all three verses you find the SAME HEBREW EXPRESSION, namely, EL GIBBOR. So here Messiah has the same title as Jehovah God.

Coming to Isaiah 40:3 we read a prophecy concerning the coming Messiah: "The voice of one that crieth in the wilderness, Prepare ye the way of Jehovah; make level in the desert a highway for our God." We find this fulfilled at John 1:23: "He [John] said, I am the voice of one crying in the wilderness, Make straight the way of the Lord, as said Isaiah the prophet." If the New Testament English were true to the Hebrew text to which it refers, it would read "the way of Jehovah," for this is the prophecy referred to which was being fulfilled. Of course it refers to Jesus Christ! So here the prophecy concerning "Jehovah . . . our God" was fulfilled by Jesus! The way was to be prepared for JEHOVAH (Isaiah 40:3); it was fulfilled by the one whom announced as "the lamb of God, that taketh away the sin of the world" (John 1:29).

Now, for the moment at least, we must pause. Otherwise, the big hand of the Watchtower will stop us. Let us face their accusations against what has been said above, and answer them. Their pretenses at accurate Bible translation will be revealed, and *The New World Translation* (the Watchtower translation of the Bible) will be exposed.

The context of Proverbs 8:22 is taken by some (including Jehovah's Witnesses) as referring to the Son of God. Regarding the Son of God, the book *Let God Be True* says on page 32: "He was the first son that Jehovah God brought forth. He is not the author of the creation; but after God had created him as his firstborn Son, then God used him . . . ." And so as the Watchtower translators made Proverbs 8:22 read: "Jehovah himself PRODUCED me as the beginning of his way." The Hebrew word QANAH translated here as *produced* has 18 different meanings, NONE OF WHICH is *produced!*

However, we find another Hebrew word, namely, QARAB, that *does* mean "produced." The Watchtower attaches the meaning of QARAB to the word QANAH, for the average Witness with his full trust in the Society would never think of questioning it! He is told that THIS is the correct translation and all others are wrong, or at the most, less accurate. He is to remain silent and not question anything the Society prints. If he gets too inquisitive, he will be closely watched and quite possibly warned that he had better mind his own business if he wishes to remain in the organization! No wonder! Look what we unearth when we investigate the Society's translation!

Let us consult Matthew Henry's *Commentary*. He believes also that the Wisdom mentioned herein is the Son of God, so this is a suitable work to quote from. From Volume III, page 835:

> The Word was eternal, and had a being before the world, before the beginning of time; and therefore it must follow that it was from eternity.
>
> *The Lord possessed him in the beginning of his way,* of his eternal counsels, for those were *before his works.* This way indeed had no beginning, for God's purposes in himself are eternal like himself, but God speaks to us in our own language. . . . The Son of God was, in the eternal counsels of God, designed and advanced to be the wisdom and power of the Father, light and life, and all in all, both in the creation and in the redemption of the world. That he *was brought forth* as to his being, and *set up* as to the divine counsels concerning his office, before the world was made, is here set forth in a great variety of expressions, much the same with those by which the eternity of God himself is expressed in Psalm 90:2, *Before the mountains were brought forth, or ever thou hadst formed the earth and the world, even from everlasting to everlasting, thou art God.*

We come to the text that gives the Witnesses the most trouble, and about which they have gone to great lengths to explain away. They have erroneously translated it in their Bible, and we are to expose the tricks they use in order to accomplish this. Most of the information is so technical that even the Witnesses cannot understand the explanation the Watchtower translators give in the appendix to the *New World Translation,* which is found on page 773. This is admittedly a matter for theologians, into which field the Witnesses have trespassed. But, since they will refer any disputant to the material in the *New World Translation* appendix (even though they can't understand it themselves), we must meet it and answer it. This we will do.

The magazine *Consolation* of November 8, 1944, in discussing *The Emphatic Diaglott*, says on page 27: "For example, the student may open the *Diaglott* at John 1:1 and read: 'In the beginning was the Logos, and the Logos was with God, and the Logos was God.' This seems to support the view of trinitarians. The minister knows that that impossible three-in-one doctrine is false; so he shift's his eye from the right-hand column to the left-hand column and reads the interlinear translation: 'In a beginning was the Word, and the Word was with the God, and a god was the Word.' This clears up the difficulty." Furthermore, Jehovah's Witnesses, in their desperation to avoid seeing what is so plain here, will point out a "difference" in the Greek text itself, even though they cannot read it! The Greek text in the *Diaglott* reads at this point: EN ARCHE EN HO LOGOS KAI HO LOGOS EN PROS TON THEON KAI THEOS EN HO LOGOS. Show this to a Jehovah's Witness the next time one of them starts on Greek and ask him to translate the above for you! He will beat a hasty retreat!

However, with the interlinear, he is able to detect that both THEON and THEOS are translated "God." He thinks that due to the difference in spelling two Gods are mentioned! This is laughable! It certainly will be a big let-down for him to find out that this is only due to the placing of the word in the sentence. We say, "I am going to the store—meet me there"; not "Me am going to the store—meet I there." So it is with the Greek sentence structure; it has its form also. In the above case both "I" and "me" refer to the same person. You cannot say there are two persons mentioned because of the two different forms of the same word used!

According to the Watchtower Bible, John 1:1 reads: "Originally (or, at a beginning) the Word was, and the Word was with God, and the Word was a god." In the appendix referred to previously, they quote (on page 768) *A Grammar of the Greek New Testament in the Light of Historical Research* by A. T. Robertson. Regarding the expression THEOS EN HO LOGOS we read their quotation from the *Grammar:* "The absence of the article here is on purpose and essential to the true idea." The "true idea" they take, naturally, to mean their perverted idea of Christ as "a god." Then on page 767 they again quote Robertson, this time giving an *incomplete* quotation as follows: "NOUNS IN THE PREDICATE. These may have the article also." No wonder they stop here! Look what follows: "AS ALREADY EXPLAINED, THE ARTICLE IS NOT ESSENTIAL TO SPEECH."

The Watchtower seems to think that if this verse were to read *"the* Word was *the* God" in Greek, they would then be free to assume that Christ is God. Let us consult Robertson's *Grammar* (on pages 767-768) regarding this problem: "It is true also that HO THEOS EN HO LOGOS *(the* God was *the* Word) would have been Sabellianism." Sabellianism is the doctrine taught by an African bishop of the 3rd century A.D., named Sabellius, that God exists as one Person, and that the Father, Son and Holy Spirit are but different manifestations of God.

This, however, would be against the Watchtower's own theory, as they hold that Jehovah and Jesus are separate persons! Not only that, but it would teach an unscriptural doctrine besides!

The Greek text at John 1:1 does NOT read *a god* regardless of anything and everything the Watchtower says to the contrary. For the benefit of those who do not read the Greek language, we will quote *A New Short Grammar of the Greek Testament* by A. T. Robertson and W. Hershey Davis. On page 274 under "No Indefinite Article in Greek" we read: "The Sanskrit and the Latin had no article of any kind (definite or indefinite) AS THE GREEK HAS NO INDEFINITE ARTICLE. Not even has the modern Greek taken up the indefinite article like that developed in the Romance and Teutonic languages."

On page 279 we read: "As a rule the article with one and

not with the other means that the articular noun is the subject. Thus HO THEOS AGAPE ESTIN can only mean 'God is love,' not 'love is God.' So in John 1:1 THEOS EN LOGOS the meaning has to be 'the Logos was God,' not 'God was the Logos.' "

On page 781 of Robertson's *Grammar* we read this interesting note: "The devil is represented as admitting that Jesus is *a* Son of God, not *the* Son of God" (Matt. 4:3, 6). This is the way Jehovah's Witnesses recognize Jesus Christ. Now we go on and quote from pages 795 and 796:

"The word 'theos' like a proper name, is freely used WITH and WITHOUT THE ARTICLE." "It would have been very easy IF THE ABSENCE OF THE ARTICLE IN GREEK ALWAYS MEANT THAT THE NOUN WAS INDEFINITE, BUT WE HAVE SEEN THAT THIS IS NOT THE CASE." (Emphasis mine). On page 790 under "The Absence of the Article" we read: "The translation of the expression INTO ENGLISH OR GERMAN is NOT DETERMINED by the MERE ABSENCE OF THE GREEK ARTICLE." (Emphasis mine).

Now we shall begin an examination of individual texts, spurred on by what we have found as a result of John 1:1. Consider Colossians 2:9. Here we find another example of Watchtower trickery. Their version of this text reads: "Because it is in him that all the fullness of the divine quality dwells for the body." Here is the text they have so translated: HOTI EN AUTO KATOIKEO PAN TO PLEROMA TES THEOTES SOMATIKOS. Some manuscripts have the word THEOTETOS in place of THEOTES. Regarding THEOTES, Thayer's *Greek Lexicon says*: "The state of being God, Godhead." Regarding THEOTETOS *The International Critical Commentary* says: "Of the Godhead." Of the word SOMATIKOS: "Bodilywise, corporeally."

The text, Colossians 2:9, is similar to Colossians 1:19 where the RSV translation reads: "For in him all the fullness of God was pleased to dwell."

Following are some translations of Colossians 2:9: "For it is in him that all the fulness of God's nature lives embodied" (*American Translation*). "Yet it is in him that God gives a full and complete expression of himself" (*Phillips*). "For it is in Christ that all the fulness of God's nature dwells embodied" (*Weymouth*). "Because in him dwells all the fullness of the Deity bodily" (*Emphatic Diaglott*). "For it is in him that all the fulness of the Deity dwells bodily" (*Moffatt* 1901). "It is in Christ that the entire fulness of deity has settled bodily" (*Moffatt* 1935). "For in Him the whole fullness of Deity (the Godhead) continues to dwell in bodily form—giving complete expression of the divine nature" (*Amplified New Testament*).

The Watchtower translation is ridiculous. It is as far from the true meaning of the Greek text as you can possibly get. Little wonder no attempt is made to explain THIS text in the *New World Translation* appendix!

Let us now consider the passage at John 8:58. Because it indicates the deity of Jesus Christ, the Watchtower alters the text. They render this passage: "Before Abraham came into existence, I have been." The expression "I have been" is taken from the Greek words EGO EIMI. At John 8:24, 28 they render this expression "I am he." In other verses they translate this "I am" (see Revelation 1:8, 17; 22:13). A footnote on John 8:58 tells us their rendering "I have been" is "properly rendered in the perfect indefinite tense." That would be fine if it were not for this one fact: THERE IS NO SUCH THING AS A "PERFECT INDEFINITE TENSE" IN THE GREEK LANGUAGE!

The reason for their dodging the issue here is obvious. There is only one "I am." At John 8:24 Jesus says: "Except ye believe that I AM (EGO EIMI) ye shall die in your sins." Then at verse 28: "When ye have lifted up the Son of man, then shall ye know that I AM (EGO EIMI)." This, of course, is JEHOVAH at Exodus 3:14, where, according to the Septuagint (Greek translation of the Old Testament) Jehovah calls Himself EGO EIMI (*I am*).

The following versions render John 8:58 as "I am": *Moffatt, Weymouth, Berkeley, Williams, Confraternity, Amplified New Testament, The New English Bible.* The Watchtower translators are guilty of deliberate, inconsistent translation in order to escape a fact they do not wish to acknowledge.

Now we will consider Hebrews 1:6. Regarding Jesus Christ, it reads: "And let all the angels of God worship him." In the *Questions From Readers* column of *The Watchtower* magazine of January 1, 1954, page 30, an article appears in answer to the question "Should we worship Jesus?" They take nearly two pages of small print to answer "No!"

Here they bring the Greek word PROSKUNEO into the picture. This is a word the New Testament uses for *worship*. In their discussion of this subject the article reads: "The knee is bent in the name of Jesus as Lord and in worship to the Father as God. . . ." Here a clear distinction is made between "Lord" and "God." Now look at this:

"Every Greek reader must confess that in the LXX (Septuagint) the Greek words *kyrios* (Lord) and *theos* (God) have been used to crowd out the name of the Supreme Deity." (Page 19, *New World Translation of the Christian Greek Scriptures*). Here the words mean the same thing!

Speaking of early copyists and their disregard for the Divine Name, the foreword reads: "In place of it they substituted the words *kyrios* (usually translated 'the Lord') and *theos,* meaning 'God.'" (*New World Translation of the Christian Greek Scriptures,* page 18).

So *The Watchtower* magazine makes a clear distinction between "Lord" and "God" while the *New World* Bible claims they stand equally for the Supreme Deity! Obviously, *The Watchtower* is trying to support a claim without evidence.

Readers of *The Watchtower* magazine apparently were not satisfied with this evasive treatment the Society was giving this subject. So, in the May 15th issue another article appeared in the same column. This time the question reverts to the answer the Society gave the first time, and asks: "Does this not contradict the statement at Hebrews 1:6?" Hebrews 1:6 reads: "And again, when he brings the firstborn into the world, he says, 'Let all God's angels worship him.'"

To this, the congenial, benevolent *Watchtower* replied: "Are you an angel of God in heaven? If you are, then Hebrews 1:6 applies to you. If you are not one of God's angels in heaven, then Hebrews 1:6 is not directed to you. . . ." Well, now! That really solves the problem completely, doesn't it? Makes it sound as if part of the Bible was written for angels and part of it for us!

Thus, we see *The Watchtower* way of avoiding the real issue. They admit the word PROSKUNEO means "worship" when it applies to Jehovah, but when it applies to Christ the meaning suddenly changes—when *people* (not angels) are called upon to "worship!"

Angels are allowed to worship God alone—see Revelation 19:10; 22:9. Yet they were called upon (Michael included, for no exceptions are made!) AT JESUS' BIRTH AS A CHILD to worship Him! Lest any think the expression "when he bringeth in the firstborn into the world" applies to some age past when He was "created," please notice that this call to worship applies when Jesus is brought into the EARTH ITSELF! Even the Watchtower translation renders the word OIKOUMENE as "INHABITED EARTH" in all fifteen times that it occurs in the New Testament! Yes, all the angels of heaven were called upon to worship (in the full sense of the word) this little Child, born into the world through Mary! At the moment of His birth He was worshiped as God!

The reasons for the Watchtower Society's decisions in these matters can more easily be understood when the reader realizes just WHO and WHAT they think Jesus was. They are not allowed to recognize him as Saviour, because their organization set-up is based upon a "work for salvation" theory. If a Saviour came, then the Watchtower treadmill would stop! The need for authoritarian control would vanish, giving way to the Holy Spirit. As it is, they have "organizational spirit" in lieu of the Holy Spirit. The "unity" they have stems from the rigid, strict control exercised by the New York headquarters over the Witnesses. The heavenly movement of the

Holy Spirit is unknown to them, for they rejected Him long ago.

Jesus told Nicodemus that he must be born again (John 3:7). Nicodemus was a sinner just as you and I. That is *why* he had to be born again. *The Watchtower* magazine of October 1, 1958, page 605, captions a paragraph "JESUS, THE FIRST TO BE BORN AGAIN." Then the paragraph remarks: "Jesus had to be born again from the spirit." Thus, they attribute to Jesus Christ the sin nature that is common to us all! But we know the Son of God, the sinless One, need not be born again.

Further, the Witnesses believe that Jesus was NOT born the Messiah! *Let God Be True* book says, page 39: "By being thus anointed with the spirit Jesus BECAME the Messiah. . . ." (Emphasis mine). The paragraph that follows says: "Jehovah God ACCEPTED him for sacrifice as mankind's Redeemer." (Emphasis mine). In other words, it was not unalterably determined what Christ should do, but merely that events so transpired that he became born again, and so was accepted as Messiah by Jehovah! If He had failed, then who would have become Messiah? I read nothing in the Scriptures about a substitute!

In sharp contrast to this, the *Bible* says: "There is born to you this day in the city of David a Saviour who IS (Greek, ESTIN) CHRIST (Greek for MESSIAH) the Lord" (Luke 2:11). If He was BORN the Messiah (as the above text states), what did He yet need to become?

Moreover, the Witnesses think that Jesus was BEGOTTEN TWICE! They believe that HE LOST HIS SONSHIP! Again quoting *Let God Be True*, page 39: "By acknowledging him as his beloved Son, God BEGOT JESUS to be his spiritual Son ONCE MORE." (Emphasis mine). Since, according to the Bible, sons of God do not have to become born again (seeing that the new birth is for the purpose of restoring sonship), we conclude therefrom, in the light of the above-quoted statement, that according to Witnesses, IT WAS NOT THE SON

OF GOD WHO BECAME MESSIAH, BUT ONLY AN EX-SON OF GOD!

The Codex Bezae and a few later manuscripts contain the clause "thou art my beloved Son, this day have I begotten thee" (Luke 3:22). This is used by persons attempting to prove that Jesus was not the Son of God in the proper sense before His baptism. The above passage has no support in older Greek manuscripts and is found only in late copies of Luke, where it is a clear gloss from Psalm 2:7.

According to the Watchtower then, it was a good man (no more than that) who became Messiah and the Son of God at the same time. This means that IT WAS NOT GOD'S SON who was thus accepted, but a good man who was taken for this position! Since they believe that Jesus could have failed (for he was just another Adam, and Adam failed!), it would be interesting to find out what they think would have happened if Jesus had decided to default.

Such, then, is the teaching of this pseudo-Christian group, parading as a recognized demonination! This is one of the most atrocious heresies ever invented by unsaved men.

Let us pursue the matter further, for the Watchtower is not yet finished with degrading Jesus. Quoting from the book *Your Will Be Done On Earth,* page 317, we read about Michael the archangel: "Michael in heaven was associated with the angel that brought the vision to Daniel." They say this in order to bolster up their teaching that Jesus was Michael! On page 316 we read: "When he died AS THE MAN JESUS CHRIST and was resurrected and went back to heaven, what was his proper name? . . . He resumed his heavenly name MICHAEL." (Emphasis mine).

The book *New Heavens and a New Earth,* page 30 says: "Michael the archangel is no other than the only-begotten Son of God, now Jesus Christ." This text seems not to bother the Watchtower: "UNTO WHICH OF THE ANGELS SAID HE AT ANY TIME, Thou art my Son, this day have I begotten thee?" (Hebrews 1:5). Once again we see the Watchtower heresy fall before the gleaming two-edged sword, the Bible (Hebrews 4:12).

So we have it: The unscriptural picture of a created angel, born later as a man who had to become born again as does any common sinner, who, at the age of thirty, became Messiah; then, after His death and resurrection, went back to become Michael the archangel again! And they call this the Christian gospel!

But let us turn from this heresy of the Watchtower to the Bible. See what it says in contrast to what we have been reading out of the Watchtower publications. A refreshing change indeed!

Consider again John 1:1. It compares with Deuteronomy 32:39: "See now that I, even I, am he, and there is no god with me." However, the reading from Bagster's Septuagint is even more significant. It reads: "Behold, behold that I am (EGO EIMI), and there is no god (THEOS) beside me." If Jesus were *a* god of any kind (as the Watchtower translation says), then something is decidedly wrong with the text. But if He were God Himself as John 1:1 concludes that He was, then the two texts harmonize.

Again we are reminded of the same expression EGO EIMI as used in John 8:24, 28, 58. *That* is why that even though John 1:1 states "the Word was WITH God," it rightly concludes by saying "the Word WAS God." Thus we have an agreement between the texts, and not a contradiction, which we would have if the Watchtower translation were accurate.

At Isaiah 44:8 Jehovah asks: "Is there a God besides me?" He answers "I know not any." This does not disturb the Witness, however, for he feels there *is* a God besides Jehovah, regardless of *what* the Scriptures say.

The Witness will make his usual feeble attempt to avoid what we are asking him to see. He will point out the difference between a small letter "g" and the capital "G," especially as he sees them used in the above texts. For his benefit we point out that in both HEBREW AND GREEK (early manuscripts) there are ONLY capital letters used!

The die-hard Jehovah's Witness has only one alternative left: He will refuse to believe the Scriptures!

Referring to Hebrews, chapter 1, from which reference has already been made, verses five and six, we follow to verse eight, where Jehovah says of the Son: "Thy throne, O God, is forever and ever." The *New World Bible* reads: "God is your throne forever." The Greek text, in reference to the Son, reads HO THEOS (THE GOD). Here we have THEOS with the definite article, speaking of the Son! Naturally the Watchtower Society never pointed THIS out to the Witnesses!

Now Titus 2:13. We find the Greek expression TOU MEGALOU THEOU KAI SOTEROS HEMON CHRISTOU IESOU. *The Watchtower* translation reads: "Of the great God and of our Saviour Christ Jesus." Reading literally as it appears word for word in Greek, we have: "OF THE GREAT GOD AND SAVIOUR OF US, CHRIST JESUS."

In the *New World* translation appendix, page 781, an attempt is made to explain their translation of this text. The reader may refer to it and draw his own conclusions. The *Revised Standard Version* reads: "Awaiting our blessed hope, the appearing of the glory of our great God and Saviour Jesus Christ." The *American Standard Version* renders it: "Looking for the blessed hope and appearing of the glory of our great God and Saviour Christ Jesus." *The Amplified New Testament:* "The glorious appearing of our great God and Saviour Christ Jesus, the Messiah, the Anointed One."

Next, we come to a text the Watchtower Society have found practically impossible to hide, though they tried. It is John 20:28 where Thomas says of Christ: HO KURIOS MOU KAI HO THEOS MOU. Which is, when translated word for word into English: "THE LORD OF ME AND THE GOD OF ME." Here again we find HO THEOS (THE GOD) used in reference to the Son! Not merely *God,* but *the* God! Needless to say, the Watchtower has no comment to make upon *this* text!

Now either Jesus IS or IS NOT what the Scriptures say He is. What do *you* say? *The Watchtower* speaks plainly, and the Bible speaks plainly. If the Watchtower is right, the Bible texts are wrong. If the Bible texts are right, then *The Watchtower Society* is wrong. Which do you choose? If you are a Jehovah's Witness, may God grant you wisdom to understand the truth as revealed in His Word concerning His only begotten Son, our Saviour, Jesus Christ.

In Isaiah 44:6 and 48:12 Jehovah declares Himself to be "the first and the last." The Witness will accept this statement but not the following ones: "I am the FIRST AND THE LAST, and the Living one; and I was dead" (Revelation 1:17, 18). "These saith the FIRST AND THE LAST, who was dead" (Revelation 2:8). At Revelation 22:13, 16, 20 we read: "I am the Alpha and the Omega, the first and the last, the beginning and the end. I Jesus have sent mine angel to testify unto you these things for the churches. I am the root and the offspring of David, the bright, the morning star. He who testifieth these things saith, Yea: I come quickly. Amen: come, Lord Jesus." "I am the Alpha and the Omega, saith the Lord, who is and who was and who is to come, the Almighty" (Revelation 1:8).

In order to avoid what can plainly be seen here, the Jehovah's Witness will say there are two "firsts" and two "lasts" and two "beginnings" and two "endings." Two "A's" to begin the alphabet and two "Z's" to end it! Thus they pit the Hebrew and Greek Scriptures against each other, creating a disagreement between the Testaments. THUS THEY SPLIT THE BIBLE INTO TWO OPPOSING FACTIONS!

Coming right down to the point, I John 5:20 says of Christ: "This is the true God" (Greek, OUTOS ESTIN HO ALETHINOS THEOS). Even the *New World* translators could not change *that!* In chapter one of Titus GOD is the Saviour in verse three; then, in verse four, JESUS is the Saviour. This compares with Isaiah 43:10 where Jehovah says: "Besides me there is no Saviour. "

Zechariah 12:10 is a text that disputants of the Trinity doctrine would like to conceal. It quotes the words of Jehovah, where He actually says: "They shall look upon ME whom they have pierced." Here the Hebrew word ALAI is used, and means "me."

Admittedly, as the *American Standard* footnote points out, a few manuscripts read *"him"* here. However, the rendering "me" is found in *all* the *ancient* Hebrew manuscripts, and not only in the best of the later ones, but also in the largest number of them. The rendering "me" is sustained by the *Septuagint, Aquila, Symmachus, Theodotian,* the *Syriac,* the *Targums,* the *Vulgate* and the *Arabic* translations. It is supported by the *Talmud* and the exposition by Rabbi Rashi. The following English translations recognize the proper translation as "me": *Douay, Harkavy, Darby, Lamsa, Berkeley Version, Rotherham, Knox, Julia Smith, Leeser, Young,* Moulton's *Modern Reader's Bible, George R. Noyes,* Dr. A. Benisch's *Jewish School and Family Bible,* Aaron Pick's *Literal Translation, The Holy Scriptures According to the Masoretic Text.* It is the fact that *Jehovah* was pierced by the soldier's spear that Paul refers to when he states that if the rulers had known His true identity "they would not have crucified the Lord of glory" (I Cor. 2:8). The footnote "s" on this passage in the *Revised Standard Version,* which states that Theodotian reads "him" has been recognized as being in error, and is being dropped from all future printings.

Now let us face the trouble that Jesus was having with the Jews over his deity. Read John 5:18: "For this cause therefore the Jews sought the more to kill him, because he not only brake the sabbath, but also called God his own Father, making himself equal with God." This is the conclusion reached by John, not that of the Jews, therefore, it is true and accurate. Note the following translations of this text and how the same thought is expressed.

"This remark made the Jews all the more determined to kill him, because not only did he break the Sabbath, but referred to God as his own Father, so putting himself on equal terms with God" (*Phillips*). "On account of this the Jews were all the more eager to kill him, because he not only broke the Sabbath, but actually called God his Father, thus putting himself on an equality with God" (*American Translation*). "The Jews therefore were all the more eager to put Him to death, because He not only broke the Sabbath, but also spoke of God as being in a special sense His Father, thus putting Himself on a level with God" (*Weymouth*). "For this reason then the Jews sought all the more to kill Him, because He was not merely breaking the Sabbath but also calling God His own 'Father,' making Himself equal to God" (*Moffat* 1901). "This made the Jews more determined than ever to kill Him, because He not only broke (weakened, violated) the Sabbath, but He actually spoke of God as being (in a special sense) His own Father, making Himself equal (putting Himself on a level) with God" (*The Amplified New Testament*).

Dear reader, do you see the inescapable fact to which this Scripture points? If this very same Jesus were upon earth today, Jehovah's Witnesses (as Unitarians and other cultists) would be His most bitter enemies! For they, like those Jews of old, will NOT accept Him as God!

In defense of His deity Jesus said: "The Son can do nothing of himself, but WHAT HE SEETH THE FATHER doing: for what things HE doeth, THESE THE SON ALSO DOETH IN LIKE MANNER" (John 5:19). Thus Jesus could equal the Father in anything He did! Take careful note, please: Jesus did NOT say He would do what he HEARD OF the Father doing, but what He SAW Him do—AND HE SPOKE THUS WHILE HE WAS IN THE FLESH UPON EARTH! thus proving His omnipresence as God. That is why we are told that He did not have to seek after equality (Philippians 2:5, 6), because HE ALREADY POSSESSED equality!

But was Jesus not *created*? Jehovah's Witnesses think He was. They quote Revelation 3:14 which reads: "These things saith the Amen, the faithful and true witness, the beginning of the creation of God." Also Colossians 1:15 which states that Jesus is "the first-born of all creation."

Regarding the texts in Colossians and Revelation we quote *Let God Be True*, page 32, paragraph 3:

This One was not Jehovah God, but was "existing in God's form." How so? He was a spirit person, just as 'God is a Spirit'; he was a mighty one, although not almighty as Jehovah God is; also he was before all others of God's CREATURES, for he was the FIRST SON that Jehovah God brought forth. Hence he is called "the only begotten Son' of God, for God had no partner in bringing forth his first-begotten Son. He was the first of Jehovah God's creations. He speaks so of himself, at Revelation 3:14: "These are the things the Amen says, the faithful and true witness, the beginning of the creation by God." (*NW*) Also at Colossians 1:15 he is spoken of as "the image of the invisible God, the firstborn of all creation." Thus he is ranked with God's creation, being first among them and also most beloved and most favored among them. (Emphasis mine.)

Matthew Henry's *Commentary* says regarding this subject:

He is the *beginning, the firstborn from the dead,* the principle, the first-born from the dead; the principle of our resurrection as well as the first-born himself. All our hopes and joys take their rise from him who is the author of our salvation. Not that he was the first who ever rose from the dead, but the first and only one who rose by his own power, and was declared to be the *Son of God, and Lord of all things.* And he is the head of the resurrection, and has given us an example and evidence of our resurrection from the dead.

The Trinity by Edward E. Bickersteth, beginning on page 105, reads:

If you regard the word *first-born* in its general acceptance among Eastern nations, it imports lordship, excellence, dignity; and as such the clause might well have been translated here, "The chief of all creation." But if you press for a more exact significance, it absolutely resists the interpretation that Christ is himself a creation of God, for then it would have been PROTOKTISIS, first created, as Chrysostom observes, not PROTOTOKOS, firstborn.

The (-TOKOS) guards against this, and the PROTO- so far from assuming him to be the first creature, declares his pre-existent priority to all creation, according to the well-known usage of the superlative for the comparative, and the clause might well have been rendered by that in our version of the Athanasian creed: "Begotten before the worlds." Thus the phrase by itself is an unambiguous testimony to his Deity; and the succeeding clauses, ascribing to him the creation of all, prove him increate; for, if a creature, he made himself, which is absurd.

Now we come to Revelation 3:14 and Bickersteth comments as follows:

> The beginning of the creation of God, HE ARCHE—Rev. 3:14. Compare with this, "I am, saith the Lord, the beginning and the end" HE ARCHE KAI TO TELOS—Rev. 21:6; 22:13. The above . . . sufficiently prove that, as used in chapter 3:14, it regards the pre-existent eternity, the "from everlasting" of the Lord, and as such declares him to be the beginning or origin, or originator, or precisely as we say, the *First Cause* of the creation of God.

Both Williams' and Goodspeed's translations of Revelation read: "The Beginner of God's creation." *The New English Bible* reads: "The prime source of all God's creation." We must also take note of Isaiah 43:10, where Jehovah says: "Before me there was NO GOD FORMED [*created,* Lamsa], neither shall there be after me."

Following are some uses of "begotten," which the Witnesses think mean "created." First Corinthians 4:15 reads: "For though ye have ten thousand instructors in Christ, yet have ye not many fathers: for in Christ Jesus I have BEGOTTEN you through the gospel." Did Paul *create* them? Philemon 10 reads: "I beseech thee for my son Onesimus, whom I have BEGOTTEN in my bonds." Did Paul *create* Onesimus? I Peter 1:3 reads: "Blessed be the God and Father of our Lord Jesus Christ, which according to his abundant mercy hath BEGOT-

TEN us again unto a lively hope by the resurrection of Jesus Christ from the dead."

Every child of God is *begotten,* but it has nothing to do with his original "creation," for his birth by nature must precede his new birth by the Spirit. I John 5:1 tells us: "Whosoever believeth that Jesus is the Christ is BEGOTTEN of God: and whosoever loveth him that begat loveth him also that is BEGOTTEN of him."

Jesus referred to His Deity when speaking of His coming resurrection: "Jesus answered and said unto them, Destroy this temple and in three days I will raise it up . . . When therefore he was raised from the dead, his disciples remembered that he spake thus" (John 2:19) .

Jehovah's Witnesses, as automatons of the Watchtower movement, can only see in the Scriptures what the Watchtower Society wants them to see. For example, at Matthew 11:27 they can readily see the words: "Neither doth any know the Father, save the Son." They think that this disproves the doctrine of the deity of Jesus. The preceding words escape their notice: "No one knoweth the Son, save the Father." It is even as He said: "The Father is in me, and I in the Father" (John 10:38) .

Concerning the resurrection of Christ, the book, *Your Will Be Done On Earth,* says on page 143: "He arose as a spirit person with a spirit body." However, *The Watchtower* is at a loss when it comes to explaining what happened to Jesus' physical body. The average Witness will say that Jehovah disposed of the body in some manner not revealed in the Bible. Well then, anything they say in that regard is merely speculation, only adding imagination contrary to the revealed report.

When Lazarus was raised from the dead, he came forth from the tomb bound in his burial garments (as bodies in those days were mummified at burial) . In Jesus' tomb, the burial garments had been removed from the body and laid neatly aside. If the Witnesses are right, why were the garments not disposed of with the body? Who was in that tomb alive, to so separate the body of Christ from its burial garments? Remember that His body had been mummified—wrapped securely and completely. Whose hands placed those wrappings where they were found, minus the body? What physical person, alive in that tomb, performed those tasks?

Following is an example of how the Watchtower translators have deliberately ADDED TO THE WORD OF GOD in order to change entirely the meaning of a passage. At I Timothy 2:6 we read of Christ "who gave himself a ransom for all." The Watchtower Bible reads "Who gave himself a CORRESPONDING ransom for all." THIS WORD CORRESPONDING IS NOT IN THE GREEK TEXT AT ALL! IT WAS DELIBERATELY ADDED TO CHANGE THE MEANING OF THE SCRIPTURE! However, even if we grant them their addition to the Word of God, we ask: What did Jesus' ransom correspond *to?* It corresponded not only to Adam, but to the entire outgrowth of Adam's sin which was atoned for. One again the Watchtower translators have failed in their attempts to conceal the truth of God's Word.

Why did these translators ever do such a thing? Well, they want the Witnesses to think that Jesus was only another Adam before the Fall, that is, a perfect man. Therefore, they took this opportunity to make it appear as if Jesus gave a ransom only of what Adam failed to give. This allows for a continuation of our own sins, not covered by Jesus' shed blood. Hence, there is only a removal of *Adam's* sin, not of ours! Through such reasoning the Watchtower Society keeps the Witnesses on that ever-turning treadmill, which is just a non-Catholic pre-death purgatory!

Following is a worthwhile quotation from William Smith's *Dictionary of the Bible,* page 3089:

> We find that when our Lord put to the Pharisees this question, "What think ye of Christ, whose Son is he?" their answer was *not,* "He is the Son of God," but "He is the Son of David;" and they could not answer the second question which he next propounded to them, "How then doth David, speaking in the Spirit, call him *Lord?*" The reason was, because the Pharisees did not expect

the Messiah to be the Son of God; and when He, who is the Messiah, claimed to be God, they rejected his claim to be the Christ.

The reason, therefore, of his condemnation by the Jewish Sanhedrin, and of his delivery to Pilate for crucifixion, was not that He claimed to be the Messiah or Christ, but because He asserted Himself to be *much more* than that: in a word, because He claimed to be the *Son of God,* and to be *God.*

This same source reads further along:

It was the claim which He put forth to be the Christ *and* Son of God, that led to our Lord's condemnation by the unaminous verdict of the Sanhedrin: "They all condemned Him to be guilty of death" (Mark 14:64; Matt. 26:63-66) ; and the sense in which He claimed to be the Son of God is clear from the narrative of John 5:18. The Jews sought the more to kill him because He not only had broken the Sabbath, but said that God was his own Father (PATERA IDION ELEGE TON THEON) , making Himself "equal unto God;"

And when He claimed Divine preexistence, saying, "Before Abraham was (GENESTHAI) , I am, then took they up stones to cast at him" (John 8:58, 59) ; and when He asserted His own unity with God, "I and the Father are *one"*—one *substance* (HEN) , not one *person* (HEIS) — "then the Jews took up stones again to stone Him" (John 10:30, 31) ; and this is evident from the words, "For a good word we stone thee not, but for blasphemy; and because that thou, being a man, makest thyself God" (John 10:33) .

Accordingly we find that, after the Ascension, the Apostles labored to bring the Jews to acknowledge that Jesus was not only the *Christ,* but was *also* a *Divine Person,* even the *Lord* Jehovah. Thus, for example, St. Peter, after the outpouring of the Holy Ghost on the day of Pentecost by Christ, says, *"Therefore* let all the house of Israel know assuredly, that God hath made that same Jesus, whom ye crucified, *both* LORD (KURIOS, JEHOVAH) *and Christ"* (Acts 2:36) . This conclusion supplies a convincing proof of Christ's God-head. *If* He is not the Son of God, equal with God, then there is no other alternative but that He was guilty of blasphemy; for He claimed "God was His own Father, making Himself equal with God," and by doing so He proposed Himself as an object of Divine worship.

And in that case He would have rightly been put to death; and the Jews in rejecting and killing Him would have been acting in obedience to the law of God, which commanded them to put to death any prophet, however distinguished he might be by the working of miracles, if he were guilty of blasphemy (Deut. 13:1-11); and the crucifixion of Jesus would have been an act of pious zeal on their part for the honor of God, and would have commended them to his favor and protection, whereas we know that it was that act which filled the cup of their national guilt, and has made them outcasts from God to this day. . . .

Those persons who now deny Christ to be the Son of God, coequal with the Father, are followers of the Jews, who, on a plea for the Divine Unity, rejected and crucified Jesus, who claimed to be God. Accordingly we find that the Ebionites, Cerinthians, Nazarenes, Photinians, and others who denied Christ's Divinity, arose from the ranks of Judaism. The Jews sinned against the comparatively dim light of the Old Testament: they who have fallen into their error reject the evidence of both Testaments. . . .

The doctrine of Christ, *the Son of God* as well as *Son of Man,* reaches from the *highest pole* of *Divine glory to the lowest pole of human suffering.* No *human mind* could *ever have devised* such a scheme as that: and when it was presented to the minds of the Jews, the favored people of God, they could not reach to *either of these two poles;*

They could not mount to the height of the Divine exaltation in Christ the *Son of God,* nor descend to the depth of human suffering in Christ the *Son of Man* . . . But in the Gospel, Jesus Christ, Son of God and Son of Man, reaches from one pole to the other, and *filleth* all

in all (Eph. 1:23). The Gospel of Christ ran counter to
the Jewish zeal for Monotheism, and incurred the charge
of Polytheism, by preaching Christ to be the Son of God,
coequal with the Father; and also contravened and challenged all the complex and dominant systems of Gentile
polytheism, by proclaiming the Divine Unity. It boldly
confronted the World, and it has conquered the World;
because 'the excellency of the power of the Gospel is not
of man, but of God' (II Cor. 4:7).

On this same subject we now quote *Basic Writings of St.
Augustine,* Vol. I, chapter 1, page 699:

> Wherefore, although we hold most firmly, concerning
> our Lord Jesus Christ, what may be called the Canonical
> rule, as it is both disseminated through the Scriptures,
> and has been demonstrated by learned . . . handlers of
> the same Scriptures, namely, that the Son of God is both
> understood to be equal to the Father according to the
> form of God in which He is, and less than the Father ac-
> cording to the form of a servant which He took; in
> which form He was found to be not only less than the
> Father, but also less than the Holy Spirit; and not only
> so, but also less even than Himself—not that Himself
> who was, but that Himself who is; because, by taking the
> form of a servant, He did not lose the form of God. . . .

Volume II, chapter 7, page 678 says:

> They say, for instance, that the Son is less than the
> Father, because it is written that the Lord Himself said,
> "My Father is greater than I." But the truth shows that
> after the same sense the Son is less also than Himself;
> for how was He not made less also than Himself, who
> 'emptied Himself, and took upon Him the form of a
> servant'? For He did not so take the form of a servant as
> that He should lose the form of God, in which He was
> equal to the Father.
>
> If, then, the form of a servant was so taken that the
> form of God was not lost, since both in the form of a
> servant and in the form of God He Himself is the same
> only-begotten Son of God the Father, in the form of God

equal to the Father, and in the form of a servant the Mediator between God and men, the man Christ Jesus; is there any who cannot perceive that He Himself in the form of God is also greater than Himself, but yet likewise in the form of a servant less than Himself?

And not, therefore, without cause the Scripture says both the one and the other, both that the Son is equal to the Father, and that the Father is greater than the Son. For there is no confusion when the former is understood as on account of the form of God, and the latter as on account of the form of a servant.

Volume II, chapter 8, page 680 on the subject "Delivering Up the Kingdom to God" reads:

Neither may we think that Christ shall so give up the kingdom to God, even the Father, as that He shall take it away from Himself. For some vain talkers have thought even this. For, when it is said, "He shall have delivered up the kingdom to God, even the Father," He Himself is not excluded, because He is One God together with the Father. But that word "until" deceives those who are careless readers of the Scriptures, but eager for controversies.

For that text continues, "For He must reign, until He hath put all enemies under His feet;" (1 Cor. 15:24, 25) as though, when He had so put them, He would no more reign. Neither do they perceive that this is said in the same way as that other text, "His heart is established: He shall not be afraid, until He see His desire upon His enemies" (Psalm 112:8). For He will not then be afraid when He has seen it. What then means, "When He shall have delivered up the kingdom to God, even the Father," as though God the Father has not the kingdom now?. . . . The words, "When He shall have delivered up the kingdom to God, even the Father," are as much as to say, When He shall have brought believers to the contemplation of God, even the Father.

For He says, "All things are delivered unto me of my Father: and no man knoweth the Son, but the Father; neither knoweth any man the Father, save the Son, and he to whomsoever the Son will reveal Him" (Matthew 11:27). The Father will then be revealed by the Son, "when He shall have put down all rule, and all authority, and all power;" that is, in such wise that there shall be no more need of any economy of similitudes, by means of angelic rulers, and authorities, and powers.

Chapter 10, page 684 reads:

In that contemplation, therefore, God will be all in all; because nothing else but Himself will be required, but it will be sufficient to be enlightened by and to enjoy Him alone . . . For we shall then contemplate God the Father and the Son and the Holy Spirit, when the Mediator between God and men, the man Christ Jesus, shall have delivered up the kingdom to God, even the Father, so as no longer to make intercession for us, as our Mediator and Priest, Son of God and Son of Man.

A significant fact is that Christ is referred to as being "after the order of Melchizedek" (Hebrews 6:20). Melchizedek was "without father, without mother, without genealogy, having neither beginning of days nor end of life, but made like unto the Son of God" (Hebrews 7:3). If Jesus had a beginning, then he could NOT be compared to Melchizedek.

Jesus, the sacrificial Lamb without blemish, was also the high priest who officiated at the sacrificial ceremony of His own slaughter. To understand the significance of this, we must go back to the time when the original sacrifices were made upon the altar. There we find (1.) The animal to be slaughtered; (2.) The high priest who performed the ceremony; (3.) The tabernacle containing the Holy of holies, into which the high priest entered to present the blood before the presence of Jehovah God.

An account of this is given in the ninth chapter of Hebrews:

Now even the first covenant had ordinances of divine service, and its sanctuary, a sanctuary of this world. For there was a tabernacle prepared, the first, wherein were the candlestick, and the table, and the setting forth of the loaves; which is called the Holy place.

And after the second veil, the tabernacle which is called the Holy of holies; having a golden altar of incense, and the ark of the covenant overlaid round about with gold, wherein is a golden pot holding the manna, and Aaron's rod that budded, and tables of the covenant; and above it cherubim of glory overshadowing the mercy-seat. Now these things having been thus prepared, the priests go in continually into the first tabernacle, accomplishing the services; but into the second the high priest alone, once in a year, not without blood, which he offereth for himself, and for the errors of the people: the Holy Spirit this signifying, that the way into the holy place hath not been made manifest, while the first tabernacle is yet standing . . .

But Christ having come a high priest of the good things to come, through the greater and more perfect tabernacle, not made with hands, that is to say, not of this creation, nor yet through the blood of goats and calves, but through HIS OWN BLOOD, entered in once for all into the holy place, having obtained eternal redemption. For Christ entered not into a holy place made with hands, like in pattern to the true; but into heaven itself, now to appear before the face of God for us.

Jesus, having made of no further value or use the original sacrifices through his own sacrifice, completely replaced the *former* ceremony. He had to be the sacrificial lamb, "a lamb without blemish and without spot" (I Peter 1:19). Also, we see from the above-quoted verses in Hebrews that he was also the high priest. At Hebrews 7:26, 27 we read: "For such a high priest became us, holy, guileless, undefiled, separated from sinners, and made higher than the heavens; who needed not daily, like those high priests, to offer up sacrifices for his own sins, and then for the sins of the people; for this he did once and for all, when he offered up HIMSELF."

Jesus was not only the lamb; He was also high priest. It was He who presented the sacrifice of the perfect lamb to

Jehovah. If *The Watchtower* theory were correct, there would have been no high priest to present the blood before Jehovah in Heaven.

Concluding our study of the deity of Jesus Christ, we quote *Let God Be True,* page 17: "When a religious organization forbids its members to read the Bible and requires its members to accept what its clergymen teach without comparing their teachings with the Holy Scriptures, such religious organization belies its claim that it is apostolic."

With those words *The Watchtower* condemns its *own* system. The *Let God Be True* book is misnamed, for it does everything *but* that! While Jehovah's Witnesses may *read* the Bible, THEY MAY NOT INTERPRET ANY PART OF IT, but are required to accept THE WATCHTOWER EXPLANATION AS THE FINAL AUTHORITY FOR INTERPRETATION! And in finality, they must accept the Watchtower translation.

But we are not yet through exposing *The Watchtower* heresy. As we continue we will consider the subject of the Triune Godhead, to give full and complete proof for the Trinity.

Chapter Three

THE TRIUNE GODHEAD

THE WATCHTOWER SOCIETY, in the book *Make Sure Of All Things* calls the Trinity "a false, unbiblical doctrine." *Let God Be True* book says, page 100: "Such a doctrine, with its attempted explanation, is very confusing." Page 102 remarks: "When the clergy are asked by their followers as to how such a combination of three in one can possibly exist, they are obliged to answer, 'That is a mystery.'"

First of all, let us consider that disputed passage, I John 5:7. The Watchtower will fight to the end in their attempt to prove that it is spurious. Naturally, there are two sides to *every* story. *The Watchtower* tells only *their* side, so we will now go to the *other* side and see what we find.

The Works of John Wesley, Volume VI, page 200, subject, *On the Trinity:*

> I dare not insist upon any one's using the word Trinity, or Person. I use them myself without any scruple, because I know of none better. But if any man has any scruple concerning them, who shall constrain him to use them? I cannot . . . I would insist only on the direct words, unexplained, just as they lie in the text: "There are three that bear record in heaven, the Father, the Word, and the Holy Ghost: And these three are one."
>
> As they lie in the text: But here arises a question: Is that text genuine? Was it originally written by the apostle, or inserted in later ages? Many have doubted of this; and, in particular, that great light of the Christian Church, lately removed to the Church above, Bengelius, —the most pious, the most judicious, and the most laborious, of all the modern commentators on the New Testament. For some time he stood in doubt of its authenticity, because it is wanting in many of the ancient

copies. But his doubts were removed by three considerations:

(1) That though it is wanting in many copies, yet it is found in more; and those copies of the greatest authority:— (2) That it is cited by a whole train of ancient writers, from the time of St. John to that of Constantine. This argument is conclusive: For they could not have cited it, had it not been in the sacred Canon:—

(3) That we can easily account for its being, after that time, wanting in many copies, when we remember that Constantine's successor was a zealous Arian, who used every means to promote his bad cause, to spread Arianism throughout the empire; and, in particular, the erasing this text out of as many copies as fell into his hands. And he so far prevailed, that the age in which he lived is commonly styled, *Seculum Arianum,—"the Arian age;"* there being then only one eminent man who opposed him at the peril of his life. So that it was a proverb, *Athanasius contra mundum: "Athanasius against the world."*

Matthew Henry's *Commentary* on I John states:

We are stopped in our course by the contest there is about the genuiness of v. 7. It is alleged that many old Greek manuscripts have it not; nor do they sufficiently inform us of the integrity and value of the manuscripts they peruse. Some may be so faulty, as I have an old printed Greek Testament so full of *errata,* that one would think no critic would establish a various lection upon. But let the judicious collators of copies manage that business. There are some rational surmises that seem to support the present text and reading.

As, (1) If we admit v. 8, in the room of v. 7, it looks too like a tautology and repetition of what was included in v. 6 . . . This does not assign near so noble an introduction of these three witnesses as our present reading does. (2) It is observed that many copies read that distinctive clause, *upon the earth: There are three that bear record upon the earth.* Now this bears a visible opposition to some witnesses elsewhere, and therefore we are told, by the adversaries of this text, that this clause must be supposed to be omitted in most books that want v. 7.

But it should for the same reason be so in all. Take we v. 6, *This is he that came by water and blood.* It would not now naturally and properly be added, *For there are three that bear record on earth,* unless we should suppose that the apostle would tell us that all the witnesses are such as are upon earth, when yet he would assure us that one is infallibly true, or even truth itself.

Following is a table of Scriptures showing the similarity of the work and acts of the Father, Son and the Holy Spirit:

THE FATHER	THE SON	THE HOLY SPIRIT
Jehovah . . . a stone of stumbling and a rock of offence. Isa. 8:13, 14	A stone of stumbling and a rock of offence. I Peter 2:8	
For who is God, save Jehovah? And who is a rock, besides our God? Psalm 18:31	The Rock was Christ. I Corinthians 10:4	Now JEHOVAH is the Spirit. II Cor. 3:17, *New World Translation*
The God of Israel said, the Rock of Israel spake to me. II Samuel 23:3	Upon this rock I will build my church. Matthew 16:18	And the SPIRIT SAID unto Philip . . . Acts 8:29; also see 10:19 and 11:12
I am the first, and I am the last. Isaiah 44:6; 48:12	I am the first and the last. Revelation 1:17, 18; see also Revelation 22:13	The ETERNAL Spirit. Hebrews 9:14
One God, the Father, of whom are all things. I Cor. 8:6	All things were made by him. John 1:3	The Spirit of God hath MADE me. Job 33:4
Do not I fill heaven and earth? saith Jehovah. Jeremiah 23:24	Lo, I am WITH you always. Matthew 28:20	Whither shall I go from thy Spirit? Psalm 139:7
Known unto GOD are all his works. Acts 15:18	Lord, THOU knowest all things. John 21:17	The SPIRIT fathoms everything. I Cor. 12:11
Him that worketh all things after the counsel of his own WILL. Ephesians 1:11	The Son WILLS to reveal him. Matthew 11:27	Dividing to everyone severally as he WILLS. I Corinthians 2:10-11

THE FATHER	THE SON	THE HOLY SPIRIT
With thee is the fountain of LIFE. Psalm 36:9	In him was LIFE. John 1:4	The Spirit is LIFE. Romans 8:10
If any man love the world, the LOVE OF THE FATHER is not in him. I John 2:15	If any man LOVE not THE LORD JESUS CHRIST. I Corinthians 16:22	I beseech you for the LOVE OF THE SPIRIT. Colossians 1:8
I will DWELL in them. II Corinthians 6:16	Christ may DWELL in your hearts by faith. Ephesians 3:17	The Spirit DWELLETH with you and shall be in you. John 14:17
No one knoweth the Son, save the Father. Matthew 11:27	No one knoweth the Father save the Son. Mathew 11:27	No one understands the thoughts of God except the Spirit of God. I Corinthians 2:11, Moffatt
I have spoken it, I will also BRING IT TO PASS. Isaiah 46:11	The revelation of Jesus Christ . . . things which must shortly COME TO PASS. Revelation 1:1	He will show you THINGS TO COME. John 16:13
I will sing of thy POWER. Psalm 59:16	With authority and POWER he commandeth. Matthew 14:21	The POWER of the Holy Spirit. Romans 15:13
In his LOVE and in his pity he redeemed them. Isaiah 63:9	I will LOVE him and manifest myself to him. Matthew 14:21	The Spirit also HELPS us in our weakness. Romans 8:26
In the beginning GOD created. Genesis 1:1	All things were made by HIM. John 1:3	The Spirit of God was hovering over the waters. Genesis 1:2
Whom GOD hath RAISED UP. Acts 2:24	Destroy this temple, and in three days I WILL RAISE IT UP. When therefore he was risen. . . John 2:18, 22	Put to death in the flesh, but QUICKENED by the Spirit. I Peter 3:18
Jehovah shall give thee rest from thy sorrow. Isaiah 14:13	Come unto me . . . and I will give you rest. Matthew 11:28	The Spirit of Jehovah caused them to rest. Isaiah 63:14

The Jehovah Witness will be ready to point out Deuteronomy 6:4, where we read: "Hear, O Israel; Jehovah our God is one Jehovah." This, he believes, will disprove the idea of a triune Godhead, who changes not (Malachi 3:6).

We find a similar passage appears in John 10:30, where

Jesus said: "I and the Father are one," not one *numerically*, but one in composite unity. The word *one* at Deuteronomy 6:4 is the same as that used in Genesis 2:24, where Adam and Eve were said to be *one* flesh. Yet they were not one numerically but one in unity.

At Exodus 6:3 we read: "And I appeared unto Abraham, unto Isaac, and unto Jacob, as God Almighty (EL SHADDAI)." The first Hebrew letter in this name is SCHIN. It has three strokes joined as one. This letter the Jews used on top of their phylacteries; it was a symbol of the Godhead, having three strokes joined together as one.

The favorite text to "prove" Jesus a creature (Colossians 1:15) has already been explained. For further enlightenment, consider the following taken from *The Interpreter's Bible:*

> The phrase *first-born of all creation* is likewise a title of dignity and function; it has nothing to do with relations of *time*. It certainly does not imply that Christ is himself a part of the creation, even the first part; the ancient church fathers rightly insist that he is called *prototokos* (first-born), not *protoktisis* (first created).
>
> The word is undoubtedly to be interpreted in the light of the royal Psalm, "I will make him my firstborn, higher than the kings of the earth" (Ps. 89:27); and more generally, in the light of the idea of the primacy of the first-born (Exod. 4:22, Jer. 31:9); the first-born is the heir and destined ruler of all. As *first-born of all creation,* Christ is accorded in respect of the created universe that place of honor and of sovereignty that belongs to the eldest son in the household or in the kingdom.

Jehovah's Witnesses object to the doctrine of the Triune Godhead because it does not conform to their reasoning. They will quote Isaiah 1:18 where we read: "Come, now, let us reason together, saith Jehovah." Apparently this is all they know of the text, so there they stop! Let us look at the *subject* of the invited reasoning, completing the verse: "Though your sins be as scarlet, they shall be white as snow;

though they be red like crimson, they shall be as wool." The Witnesses ignore the latter part of the text, because the offer of salvation full and free through the shed blood of Jesus Christ is not part of their doctrine.

Other translations of the above-quoted text read: "Then come—let our controversy be brought to issue, saith the Lord" (Thomson's translation of the *Septuagint*). "Come, let me put it thus, the Eternal argues" (*Moffatt*, 1935). There is no talking back in defiance of Jehovah. "For who hath known the mind of the Lord? or who hath been his counsellor?" (Romans 11:34).

A triune invocation is given to God at Revelation 4:8. Here the Vatican Manuscript #1209 has "holy" *nine* times—that is, "Holy, holy, holy" for each Person of the Trinity. Note also the three titles of God at Revelation 22:13. As for the expression "My Father is greater than I," which the Witnesses use to "prove" Jesus' "inferiority" to the Father, note the following: Philippians 2:5-11 shows that Jesus was obedient unto *death* on the Cross. After that His subjection is gone. Prior to His death and resurrection He had divested Himself of all His heavenly glory and, playing the part of man, was subject to the Father. Afterward He again had His equal status with the Father.

We must now take note of the following, taken from *Let God Be True* book, page 109:

> However, the trinitarian teachers will have several embarrassing questions to answer on this text, such as, Whose voice came from heaven, saying, "This is my beloved Son"? Jesus' own voice? And where, till then, had the "Holy Ghost" or holy spirit been, seeing that first now it descended upon Jesus? And were not the heavens open to Jesus, if God, during the previous thirty years of his earthly sojourn? If he was God or part of a trinity and equal in power, substance and eternity with God, he would always have access to the heavens. These and other equally embarrassing questions have convinced the clergy that it is far better to say it is all a great mystery.

The final paragraph in the chapter sums up by saying: "No, there is no trinity!"

To answer the first question we say: It was the voice of God the Father speaking from heaven. He spoke to God the Son. The Father was in heaven while the Son was upon earth.

Where was the Holy Spirit until then? Please note that it does *not* say that this was the first "meeting" of Jesus and the Spirit. It was a rare visible manifestation of the Holy Spirit. The Trinity was fully evident there, the second and third Persons being visible.

Jesus did not *need* the Holy Spirit to descend upon Him in the Witness sense of need in order to begin His public ministry. He did NOT say He needed the Holy Spirit in order to become born again, as the Watchtower Society claims He did! He was not weak and unendowed with the Holy Spirit as any mere sinner.

As for Heaven opening, note that it does *not* say that it opened for *Jesus,* but rather, for the *Holy Spirit!* "The heaven was opened, and the Holy Spirit descended" (Luke 3:21, 22 *New World* and *Weymouth* translations).

Where was God while Jesus was in His grave? Jehovah (God the Father) in His glory never vacated the heavenly throne. Jesus (God the Son), was divested of His glory while upon earth. Hence Mary could exclaim, "My soul extols the Lord, and my spirit triumphs in God my Saviour," while the Saviour was yet in her womb! (Luke 1:46, *Weymouth*).

We have already mentioned Isaiah 48:16. An examination of the context (verses 12 to 16) will disclose to any Jehovah's Witness the fact that he knows absolutely nothing about the Jehovah mentioned therein! He knows a *Watchtower Jehovah,* but not the *Bible Jehovah.* According to Bagster's *Septuagint,* verse 16 reads: "And now the Lord God (KURIOS KURIOS) has sent me and the Spirit there." In our Hebrew texts the expression KURIOS KURIOS is ADON YAHWEH, or "The Lord Yahweh (Jehovah)."

The Witness will look at Isaiah 48 and say that it is Isaiah

who is speaking. If he does this, he then makes Isaiah "the
first and the last" who "laid the foundation of the earth!"
(verses 12 and 13).

Note the terms used in baptism. It is in the *name* (singular) of the Father, Son and Holy Spirit that we are to be
baptized. Philippians 2:9 says the name Jesus is above every
other name!

The only early "church father" whom Jehovah's Witnesses
will accept is Arius. H. G. Wells' *Outline of History,* Vol. I,
page 546 says: "Arius, for example, is accused of adopting
heretical opinions because he was not appointed Bishop of
Alexandria . . . Most of the barbarian invaders of the empire
were Arians probably because their simple minds found the
Trinitarian position incomprehensible."

Since comment by the Watchtower Society on Scriptures
as those used above are rare indeed, the Witness will be
forced to interpret them himself, and this he is not prepared
to do! He has only one other alternative: He may *reject* the
Scriptures, since they do not conform to his Watchtower theology. He moves away from the Bible and back to the Society; back to the fear of the ruling body; back to Watchtower
organization-mindedness.

It is plain that the Bible and *The Watchtower Society* are
at extreme opposite sides in this issue. We have seen the
deceitful mistranslation of the Watchtower Bible translation
exposed in its attempts to keep the truth from the people.
We have likewise exposed the deceitful writings of *The
Watchtower* publications, designed to keep the people from
studying the Bible itself, that is, without the necessity of
Watchtower books designed to influence their thinking.

Millions of people have been deceived into believing that
this is an honest, upright, straightforward Bible publication
Society! We shall have more to say about this later on.

The Jehovah's Witness is so impressed by the organization
that he will not give it up, not even when faced with this
array of evidence against it. Why? Fear! Fear of the organization!

The Jehovah's Witness so fears the organization, that he believes if he leaves it, all recourse to God will have been cut off. He believes it is his only opportunity to work out his salvation. He believes that if he leaves the organization he will have no further access to "truth." The Society long ago talked him out of finding truth in the Bible alone. They made him seek it from the organization alone, and he still does. That is the pitiful state of one who has had all individuality destroyed. He sees and thinks *organization* only.

The following chapter now delves into the system of organizational works versus salvation, full and free. The Jehovah's Witness is never told the *price* of salvation. This is to keep him on the Watchtower treadmill, working for a salvation that he never gets. But now for a complete discussion, let us move on into the next chapter.

Chapter Four

WORKING OUT SALVATION—HOW
GREAT THE PRICE?

NOW WE FACE THE QUESTION: ARE JEHOVAH'S WITNESSES ALLOWED SALVATION? The answer is, No! Neither now nor on the deathbed. There is no room in their theology for the assurance of salvation of a born-again believer.

Speaking of sin and the price for its removal, the book *From Paradise Lost to Paradise Regained* says on page 143: "However, God could arrange for the price to be paid by another who was willing and able to do so. In this way those who suffered wrongly because of Adam's sin could have AN OPPORTUNITY for life" (Emphasis mine). Notice it is not suffering for OUR OWN sins, but only Adam's. Also it is not LIFE, but an OPPORTUNITY!

Now on page 241 we read these discouraging words: "Now what have we learned about judgment? We have learned that a person could fall away and be judged unfavorably either now or at Armageddon, or during the thousand years of Christ's reign, or at the end of the final test."

Here, in a nutshell, is their formula for salvation: First, page 242 of the same book: "First, if you want to receive God's blessings you must study his Bible." Now on to page 244: "What is the second of the things you must do to get ready for life in the new paradise? You must meet with other people who have this same knowledge and faith." Then, page 246: "The third thing that you must do in order to receive God's favor is to change your living from the former way to God's way."

Note that all of this is NOT for salvation, but for "God's blessings" and/or "favor." In order to get people to believe all this a door-to-door routine is required, selling books printed by the Watchtower Society. Page 249 says: "We have to do more than merely accept the kingdom message. . . . We must also publicly declare that Kingdom to others." Their final word of advice on how to get started in this book-selling career is found on page 250: "Follow him by dedicating yourself." What they mean is, dedicate yourself to a career of bookselling and indoctrinating others even as you yourself have been indoctrinated.

To discourage the Witnesses from entertaining hopes of a present and lasting salvation, the book *Make Sure Of All Things* under the subject, "Salvation" raises this question on page 332: "If 'Once Saved Always Saved,' Why Did God Reject Israel Whom He Saved From Egypt?" They then quote their favorite text (taken out of its context, of course), Philippians 2:12: "Work out your own salvation with fear and trembling."

In this book they make an interesting statement on page 336: "To Jehovah the Saviour-God belongs all credit for salvation." At Titus 1:3, 4 we find that *Jesus* is the Saviour-God! If the Witnesses deny Jesus as Saviour, they deny Him as Messiah, or Christ. Yet if they admit Him to be the Christ, then they have to admit Him to be the Saviour-God Jehovah! That is why you will never get a direct answer from a Jehovah's Witness on this question.

The Bible way of salvation is vastly different from the salvation-by-works plan of the Watchtower. If you ask a Witness whether or not he is saved, he cannot give you a straightforward answer. He will say, "Well, I hope to be saved eventually." Or, "If I die faithful I have a chance to come back in the New World." Or again, "As long as I stay in the organization I have a chance to go through Armageddon, for the *organization* will be spared, not *individuals*." The Jehovah's Witness does not believe one can *lose* salvation, because he does not believe salvation can be possessed here and now.

Let us look at the Biblical promise of salvation that Jesus

Christ brought down. In Isaiah 53 we find that Messiah was to accomplish the following: Bear our griefs and sicknesses; be wounded for our transgressions; become bruised for our iniquities and be chastised for us; Jehovah would lay *our* iniquity on him; He would bear our sin and intercede for us as transgressors.

A promise of Messiah's deliverance was also found in the time of Moses, when deadly serpents were sent throughout the land, taking the lives of the people. "And Jehovah said unto Moses, Make thee a fiery serpent, and set it upon a standard: and it shall come to pass, that every one that is bitten, when he seeth it, shall live. And Moses made a serpent of brass, and set it upon the standard: and it came to pass, that if a serpent had bitten any man, when he looked unto the serpent of brass, he lived," Numbers 21:8, 9. This was not a salvation by good works, but by faith.

We read in John 3:14, 15: "And as Moses lifted up the serpent in the wilderness, even so must the Son of man be lifted up: that whosoever *believeth in* him . . . may have eternal life." How plain and simple! Far different from the salvation by works as taught by the Witnesses is the salvation by the grace of God as taught by the Bible.

"Surely there is not a righteous man upon earth, that doeth good, and sinneth not" (Ecclesiastes 7:20). " Your iniquities have separated between you and your God, and your sins have hid his face from you, so that he will not hear" (Isaiah 59:2). "Yet thou saidst, I am innocent; surely his anger is turned away from me. Behold, I will enter into judgment with thee, because thou sayest, I have not sinned" (Jeremiah 2:35). You are free from the law you say, and therefore have not broken it? "For as many as have sinned without the law shall also perish without the law: and as many as have sinned under the law shall be judged by the law" (Romans 2:12).

In their publications within the last few years, the Watchtower Society has recommended a self-eradication of sin. They teach that we can control over sin; that sin is only made up of bad habits, which, when constantly practiced, wear permanent "circuits" into our nervous system. They suggest that a gradual elimination of these practices will remove the "circuits." Their method for accomplishing this is, of course, performing works for their organization. They suggest that such works thereby become works of righteousness, which will count up toward a treasure, which treasure could add up to salvation. Of course, this salvation is never fully paid for, so a follower can *never* get off the Watchtower treadmill!

To answer their favorite text on this subject, Philippians 2:12, note please the verse that follows: "For it is GOD WHO WORKETH IN YOU both to WILL AND TO WORK, for his good pleasure." We see that it is GOD who is performing works, not man. God is at work through those ALREADY SAVED. Christians perform works BECAUSE they are saved, NOT in order to BE saved. By good works man cannot possibly save himself. "For we are all become as one that is unclean, and all our righteousnesses are as a polluted garment: and we all do fade as a leaf; and our iniquities like the wind, take us away" (Isaiah 64:6).

In this regard please see Romans 4:1-16. Jehovah's Witnesses can offer nothing, of course, to a dying man. If a dying man wanted to repent and be saved, the Jehovah's Witness would stand by with helpless hands, with no hope to offer. His technique is a long drawn-out process of debating and distributing Watchtower literature. And so, no hope for a dying man! Only for those capable of PRODUCING for the Watchtower theocratic-machine are given any reason to hope that they will finally be saved. There is no way of salvation to offer to a dying man.

There is no grace, no free salvation for anybody who believes. The Jehovah's Witness has a secret fear which he keeps hidden in his heart—the fear never expressed, the fear of the Watchtower authority. Rather he should have a greater fear of coming judgment by God. "We shall all stand before the judgment-seat of God" (Romans 14:10). *Weymouth* reads: "We shall all stand at the bar of God." II Corinthians 5:10 expresses the warning: "For we must all of us appear before Christ's judgment-seat in our true characters, in order that each may then receive an award for his actions in this life" (*Weymouth*).

The Witness is taught that these doctrines are not true. The Watchtower tells him that we have no souls and that we will never have to face God's final judgment.

The salvation that Jesus brought removes fear of judgment, for "there is therefore now NO CONDEMNATION to them that are in Christ Jesus" (Romans 8:1). Why not? Because "he that heareth my word, and believeth him that sent me, HATH ETERNAL LIFE, and cometh NOT INTO JUDGMENT, but hath PASSED OUT OF DEATH INTO LIFE" (John 5:24). "He that hath the SON HATH [present possession] the life; he that hath NOT the Son of God hath NOT the life" (I John 5:12).

Man cannot work for his salvation by going from door to door with the Watchtower message. Only "the blood of Jesus . . . cleanseth us from all sin" (I John 1:7). Jesus told Nicodemus that he must be "born again" (John 3:7). He said this new birth came by the Spirit (John 3:8). Without the new birth, there remains nought but the fear of judgment coming (Hebrews 10:27).

The elect of God (Romans 8:28-33) are, according to Paul 1) Predestinated; 2) Called; 3) Justified; 4) Glorified. It is therefore God who has chosen us. The Watchtower relegates all Jehovah's Witnesses to the servant or slave "class" (thus making them *Watchtower* slaves.) They use Luke 17: 10 as a basis: "Even so ye also, when ye shall have done all things that are commanded you, say, We are unprofitable servants; we have done that which it was our duty to do." However, this text according to the *Weymouth* translation reads: "So you also, when you have obeyed all the orders given you, must say, 'There is no merit in our service: what we have done is only what we were in duty bound to do.'" This does not teach that we should be "Watchtower slaves," for works do not count for salvation! We are told at John 15:15, 16: "NO LONGER DO I CALL YOU SERVANTS; for the servant knoweth not what his Lord doeth: but I HAVE CALLED YOU FRIENDS . . . YE DID NOT CHOOSE ME, BUT I CHOSE YOU."

I Corinthians 6:20 and 7:23 tells us "Ye were bought with a price." Since we are the purchase of someone else, we are not our own. The debt of sin has been cancelled on our behalf, and the redeemed are now free. The sinless Lord Jesus Christ paid it all for us. "If therefore the Son shall make you free, ye shall be free indeed" (John 8:36). "For freedom [not slavery] did Christ set us free: stand fast therefore, and BE NOT ENTANGLED again IN A YOKE OF BONDAGE" (Galatians 5:1).

We are considered "crucified with Christ" (Romans 6:6) when we are redeemed, or born again. Also, "If we died with Christ, we believe we shall also live with him" (Romans 6: 8). Therefore "being made free from sin, ye became servants of righteousness" (Romans 6:18). So, "Now being made free from sin and become servants of God, ye have your fruit unto sanctification, and the end eternal life" (Romans 6:22). Where shall we spend this eternity? Jesus said, "I go and prepare a place for you, I COME AGAIN, and will receive you UNTO MYSELF; that WHERE I AM, THERE YE MAY BE ALSO" (John 14:3). Where did He go? "My Father's house," he said (John 14:2).

This promise we can claim only by *faith*, not by *works*. This is definitely told at Romans 4:2-8, 16, 23-25: "If Abraham was justified by works, he hath whereof to glory; BUT NOT TOWARD GOD. For what saith the Scripture? And Abraham believed God, and it was reckoned unto him for righteousness. Now to him that WORKETH, THE REWARD IS NOT RECKONED AS OF GRACE, BUT AS OF DEBT." In other words, if by works, salvation would be merely wages paid for the work performed. But it is a free gift by grace.

"But to him that WORKETH NOT, but BELIEVETH ON HIM that justifieth the ungodly, HIS FAITH is reckoned for RIGHTEOUSNESS. Even as David also pronounceth blessing upon the man, unto whom God reckoneth RIGHTEOUSNESS APART FROM

WORKS, saying, Blessed are they whose iniquities are forgiven, and WHOSE SINS ARE COVERED." Why is it so?

"For this cause it is of faith, THAT IT MAY BE ACCORDING TO GRACE" (v. 16). Abraham looked FORWARD TO the redemption by Messiah; we look BACKWARD TO His death on the cross for us. "Now it was not written for his sake alone, that it was reckoned unto him; but FOR OUR SAKE ALSO, unto whom it shall be reckoned, WHO BELIEVE on him that raised Jesus our Lord from the dead, who was DELIVERED UP FOR OUR TRESPASSES, and was RAISED FOR OUR JUSTIFICATION" (4:23-25). And so "being now justified BY HIS BLOOD shall we be SAVED FROM THE WRATH OF GOD THROUGH HIM" (5:9).

Again we are reminded of the "church father" Arius of Jehovah's Witnesses. Their view of Christ and salvation stems from this source, which is a perverted view of Christ which, in turn leads to a perverted view of salvation. The Jehovah's Witness position partakes of this perversion. The following quotation is taken from James Hastings' *Encyclopedia of Religion and Ethics,* Volume I, page 781, under the subject *Arianism:*

> Despite all the efforts of Arius to popularize his opinions, they never found favour with the people. The movement was clerical rather than lay; the difficulties it sought to overcome were those of Origenist theologians perplexed by philosophical doubts and seeking an explanation where none was possible. Nor did Arianism pure and simple ever fail to arouse a strong feeling of indignation; the creed of Arius and Eunomius Sirminian "blasphemy," the opinions of Arius and Eunomius all caused a storm.
>
> It was only by insinuating itself in the plausible guise of Scriptural phraseology that Arianism ever obtained a hearing. Nor could it be otherwise. An Arian Christ, a created Logos unable to reveal an unknown God, could never be the Christ acknowledged by Christians as the Incarnate Word, the sole Mediator between God and man, the supreme Sacrifice for the sin of the world. . . . Arianism does not seem to have sprung from any strong

ethical impulse. Its philosophy was pagan, and the object of its leaders was political rather than religious.

Quoting the same authority, page 786:

> Arianism declared God to be unknowable, and the Son completely detached from Him. Humanity can therefore never be brought by Christ to the truly Divine, but only to a sort of pseudo-divinity created in the Son by the Father. . . .
>
> If Jesus Christ existed from eternity, and is Head of a kingdom which shall have no end, if He is indeed to be worshipped and received as God, then the Nicene doctrine is true, and He is of one substance with the Father. Otherwise, Christians have been mistaken from the first in their conception of Him, and He is not Divine, but a creature. . . .

Such is the source of the present-day Jehovah's Witness teachings. Consider that when this "new truth" is presented to you, it is old heresy, *not* new truth!

It is with joy and thanksgiving that the redeemed receive the words, "The law of the Spirit of life in Christ Jesus made me free from the law of sin and death" (Romans 8:2). And so "ye are not in the flesh but in the Spirit, IF SO BE THAT the Spirit of God dwelleth in you. But if any man HATH NOT the Spirit of Christ, HE IS NONE OF HIS" (Romans 8:9).

We cannot overemphasize the danger of the Arian heresy. The Bible warns us to steer clear of such teaching. The *Schaff-Herzog Encyclopedia*, Volume I, page 281, says:

> REFUTATION OF ARIANISM: On the other hand, Arianism was refuted by Scriptural passages, which teach directly or indirectly the divinity of Christ, and his essential equality with the Father. The conception of a created Creator, who existed before the world, and yet himself began to exist, was shown to be self-contradictory and untenable.
>
> There can be no middle between Creator and creature; no time before the world, as time is itself a part of the world, or the form under which it exists successive-

ly; nor can the inchangeableness of the Father, on which
Arius laid great stress, be maintained, except on the
ground of the eternity of his Fatherhood, which, of
course, implies the eternity of the Sonship. . . .

Athanasius charges Arianism with dualism, and even
polytheism, and with destroying the whole doctrine of
salvation. For if the Son is a creature, man still remains
separated, as before, from God: no creature can redeem
other creatures, and unite them with God.

We stress the above because of its relation to the doctrine
of salvation. A creature-Christ cannot save. No matter how
much Jehovah's Witnesses insist they believe on Jesus Christ,
their faith is vain because no such creature-Christ exists.

Unless a person is willing to see Christ as Thomas did, as
his Lord and God, he will seek Him in vain. You either
come God's way for salvation or you do not arrive.

"For as many as are LED BY THE SPIRIT of God, THESE ARE
the sons of God" (Romans 8:14). The sweet, mystical union
of His Spirit with our spirit (neither of which exists, according to Jehovah's Witnesses!) tells us so. "The Spirit himself beareth witness with our spirit, that we ARE children of
God" (Romans 8:16).

Answering *Make Sure Of All Things* on the subject of
losing one's salvation, note that God destroyed ONLY those
Israelites who REFUSED TO BELIEVE (Jude 5). Regarding Hebrews 3:17 which the Witnesses use in their attempt to
"prove" one's salvation can be lost, note that those whose
bodies fell in the wilderness were of the original generation
which began the journey, who would not *believe* God despite
all the signs He gave them (Numbers 14:11).

Recall the words of Paul regarding those saved. He said
that absolutely *nothing* could cause the believer to fall away
once he was truly saved (Romans 8:38, 39). "Being confident
of this very thing, that he who began a good work in you
WILL perfect it until the day of Jesus Christ" (Philippians
1:6). Paul expressed no doubt about it at all!

Jesus Christ is the author of our eternal salvation (Hebrews 5:9). Therefore HE was the full PRICE ALREADY PAID for our salvation. If He paid only part of the price and we must pay the rest, then His was not a REDEMPTIVE sacrifice. However, the price He paid needs no adding to (by works or otherwise), "Concerning which salvation the prophets sought and searched diligently, who prophesied of the grace that should come unto you" (I Peter 1:10). When Jesus said, "It is finished" (John 19:30), He was speaking of that redemption which He came to earth to provide (Luke 19:10). He FINISHED the work!

Again refer to the words of Paul, "for the grace of God hath appeared, bringing salvation to all men" (Titus 2:11). How? "According to his MERCY he saved us, THROUGH THE WASHING OF REGENERATION AND RENEWING OF THE HOLY SPIRIT" (Titus 3:5).

And so the redeemed can join Paul, "Henceforth there IS laid up for me the crown of righteousness, which the Lord, the righteous judge, SHALL GIVE ME AT THAT DAY [positive words, these!]; and not to me only, BUT ALSO TO ALL THEM THAT HAVE LOVED HIS APPEARING" (II Timothy 4:8).

As it is, not all love His appearing (at the second Coming). Jehovah's Witnesses do not even look forward to it. They scoff at the very thought of it. What fate awaits persons who continue like this till death? Eternal punishment. And even at this fact the Jehovah's Witness mocks and scoffs.

One thing is certain: When they awake in that place they refuse to believe in, it will suddenly be a matter of mockery no more! *Then* they will wish that they had believed God's Word while they were yet in this present life! But then it will be too late!

Stop and think, Jehovah's Witness: What if it *is* true, after all? What then?

Chapter Five

ETERNAL PUNISHMENT—FOR WHOM AND WHERE?

THE WATCHTOWER SOCIETY teaches that the body is the soul, and it is annihilated at death. They deny any punishment beyond that. Let us turn to their official publications for statements on this subject. The booklet entitled *Hope* has this to say on page 17:

> When those called "Protestants" broke away from the Roman Catholic organization they rejected the "purgatory" doctrine, but held on to many others of its doctrines, including a "hell of torment in fire and brimstone." The "Protestants" teach that at death of the wicked, those not church members, the soul leaves the body and is immediately consigned to such religious "hell," to suffer there eternally, without escape. When told that such would be a gross injustice to the creature, those religionists quote the words of one of Job's three tormentors: "Shall mortal man be more just than God?" (Job 4:17) ... Jehovah is a God of perfect justice, and therefore he does not subscribe to any such doctrine or arrangement of conscious torment of creatures.

From page 32 of this booklet, we read:

> Religion's doctrine of temporary or eternal torment after man's death is based upon a fundamental lie, and hence cannot be true.

Regarding the subject of Gehenna, about which we shall deal later, the booklet says, page 28:

> The fire-lit valley of Hinnom, or "Gehenna of fire," is otherwise spoken of as "a lake of fire burning with brimstone," into which the demonized opposers of Je-

hovah's THEOCRATIC GOVERNMENT by Christ Jesus are cast and destroyed.

Then this enlightening statement on page 38:

> Where, then, are the dead? Religion has blinded the dupes of the demons so that they cannot see the plain and simple answers to these questions and which the all-wise God gives in his Word.

The Watchtower magazine of February 15, 1954 discusses the subject of "The Rich Man and Lazarus" found in Luke, chapter 16, page 109, paragraph No. 2:

> Granting, for the sake of argument, that his listeners did think it was an actual incident, that, far from proving that it was, proves just the opposite. How so? Because we are explicitly told that the reason Jesus spoke in parables or illustrations was—that people might understand?—no, but that they might NOT understand. Note his words: "To you it is granted to understand the sacred secrets of the kingdom of God, but for the rest it is in illustrations, in order that, though looking, they may look in vain, and though hearing, they may not get the meaning." (Luke 8:10 *NW*) Obviously, whatever meaning his listeners got from the illustration WAS BOUND TO BE THE WRONG ONE (Emphasis mine).

Yet He told the apostles "to you it is granted to understand," but that does not convince the Watchtower.

The fact that the Bible does not say this account is a parable does not prevent *The Watchtower* from making it a parable. If it suits their convenience, it becomes a parable. What reasons do they offer? The same issue of *The Watchtower* on page 111 says:

> According to the Scriptures heaven and Hades (Sheol) are at opposite extremes. (Ps. 139:8; Luke 10:15.). Could we imagine those in one place seeing those in the other and carrying on a conversation? And were the rich man in a burning hell would he ask for just a drop of water to cool his tongue? How much relief

would that bring? Would it last to reach him? Could anyone get anywhere near a burning hell with just a drop of water? Obviously this is a figure of speech even as is Abraham's bosom, yes, and as are all the rest of Jesus' words on that occasion.

Since the Bible says, Hebrews 9:27: "And inasmuch as it is appointed unto men once to die, and AFTER THIS COMETH JUDGMENT," we had better look carefully into the Scriptures to see what they teach.

A favorite text of the Witnesses is Genesis 2:7, which satisfies them that there will never be any judgment after death. It reads: "And Jehovah God formed man of the dust of the ground, and breathed into his nostrils the breath of life; and man became a living soul." They hold that "soul" means only physical life. Now here is what they do not know: The Hebrew words involved in this text are: ". . . breathed (NEPHACH) into his nostrils the breath (NESHAMAH) of life; and man became a living soul (NEPHESH CHAI)." The word NESHAMAH used here is the same word found at Isaiah 57:16 for SOUL: "For I will not contend for ever, neither will I be always wroth; for the spirit would faint before me, and the SOULS that I have made."

The Hebrew word CHAI has 11 meanings; it is translated *living* 73 times. The word NEPHESH has 22 meanings, being translated *person* 30 times. So we see from the way the above verse is constructed that Jehovah breathed into man the NESHAMAH (SOUL) of life, and man became a LIVING PERSON (NEPHESH CHAI). In harmony with this Jehovah is called "the God of the spirits of all flesh" at Numbers 16:22, again showing that man is more than just body.

Along this same line consider Psalm 143:3 and Lamentations 3:6. The texts being similar, we will quote just the one (Psalms): "For the enemy has persecuted my soul; He hath smitten my life down to the ground: He hath made me to dwell in dark places, as those that have been long dead." He likened his being made to dwell in "dark places" as that of the condition of the dead. He was alive and *consciously* dwelling in those "dark places." He was not extinct or annihilated while there, and he indicated the "dead" are in the same condition!

Again, consider Jesus' words as recorded at Matthew 22: 31, 32: "But as touching the resurrection of the dead, have ye not read that which was spoken unto you by God, saying, I am the God of Abraham, and the God of Isaac, and the God of Jacob? God is not the God of the dead, but of the living."

Here are noteworthy portions of Matthew Henry's *Commentary*, Vol. V, page 323:

> Now the drift of the argument is to prove, (1.) That there is a future state, another life after this, in which the righteous shall be truly and constantly happy. This is proved from what God said; *I am the God of Abraham* . . . (2.) That the soul is immortal, and the body shall rise again, to be united; if the former point be gained, these will follow; but they are likewise proved by considering the time when God spoke this; it was to Moses at the bush, long after Abraham, Isaac and Jacob were dead and buried; and yet God saith not "*I was*," or "*have been*," but, *I am the God of Abraham.* Now *God is not the God of the dead, but of the living* . . . If, when Abraham died, there had been an end of him, there had been an end likewise of God's relation to him as his God; but at that time, when God spoke to Moses, he was the God of Abraham, and therefore Abraham must then be alive; which proves the immortality of the soul in a state of bliss; and that, by consequence, infers the resurrection of the body; for there is such an inclination in the human soul to its body, as would make a final and eternal separation inconsistent with the bliss of those that have God for *their* God. The Sadducee's notion was, that the union between body and soul is so close, that, when the body dies, the soul dies with it . . . *Lastly,* We have the issue of this dispute. The Sadducee's were *put to silence* (v. 34), and so put to shame.

Just what is the historic doctrine of Hell that Jehovah's

Witnesses deny? We shall now look into this teaching which the Church has held for nearly 2000 years. A quotation of Professor Samuel C. Bartlett in Dr. William Smith's *Dictionary of the Bible,* on the subject of *Hell,* page 1039:

> *Sheol,* the unknown region into which the dying disappeared, was naturally and always invested with gloom to a sinful race. But the vague term was capable of becoming more or less definite according to the writer's thought. Most commonly it was simply the grave, as we use the phrase; sometimes the state of death in general; sometimes a dismal place opposed to heaven, e.g., Job 11:8; Ps. 139:8; Amos 9:2; sometimes a place of extreme suffering, Ps. 86:13; 9:17; Prov. 23:14. No passage in the O. T., we believe, implies that the spirits of the good and bad were brought together. The often cited passage (Isa. 14:9) implies the contrary, showing us only the heathen kings meeting another king in mockery.
>
> To translate this Hebrew term, the LXX adopted the nearest Greek word, Hades, which by derivation signifies the invisible world. But the Greek word would not carry Greek notions into Hebrew heology. When Christ and his Apostles came, they naturally laid hold of this Greek word already introduced into religious use. But, of course, they employed it from their own standpoint. And as it was the purpose of their mission to make more distinct the doctrine of retribution, and as under their teachings death became still more terrible to the natural man, so throughout the N. T. Hades seems invariably viewed as the enemy of man, and from its alliance with sin and its doom, as hostile to Christ and his church. In many instances it is with strict propriety translated "hell." Even in Acts 2:27, 31 quoted from the O. T., Hades is the abode of the wicked dead. In Luke 16:23 it certainly is the place of torment. In Matt. 16:18 it is the abode and centre of those powers that were arrayed against Christ and his church. In Luke 10:5, Matt. 11:15, it is the opposite of heaven.
>
> The word occurs, according to the Received Text, in I Cor. 15:55; but the reading is not supported by the old-

er MSS. The only remaining instances are the four that occur in Rev. 1:18; 6:8; 20:13, 14 where, though in three of these cases personified, it is still viewed as a terror to man and a foe to Christ and his kingdom, over which at length he has gained the victory. While therefore *Gehenna* is the term which most distinctly designates the place of future punishment, *Hades* also repeatedly is nearly its equivalent; and notwithstanding the greater vagueness of the terms, it remains true, as Augustin asserts, that neither *Hades* or *Sheol* are ever used in good sense, or (we may add) in any other than a sense that carries the notion of terror.

What about this subject of Gehenna? *The Watchtower Society* said in the *Hope* booklet, previously quoted, that Gehenna is where all non-Jehovah's Witnesses go. Smith's *Bible Dictionary,* page 879 says:

> The "valley of Hinnom," or "of the son," or "children of Hinnom" (A. V.), a deep narrow glen to the South of Jerusalem, where, after the introduction of the worship of the fire-gods by Ahaz, the idolatrous Jews offered their children to Molech (2 Chr. 28:3; 33:6; Jer. 7:31; 19:2-6). In consequence of these abominations the valley was polluted by Josiah (2 Kings 23:10); subsequently to which it became the common lay-stall of the city, where the dead bodies of criminals, and the carcasses of animals, and every other kind of filth was cast, and, according to late and somewhat questionable authorities, the combustible portions consumed with fire. From the depth and narrowness of the gorge, and perhaps, its ever-burning fires, as well as from its being the receptacle of all sorts of putrefying matter, and all that defiled the holy city, it became in later times the image of the place of everlasting punishment, "where their worm dieth not, and the fire is not quenched;" in which place the Talmudists placed the mouth of hell: "There are two palm-trees in the Valley of Hinnom, between which a smoke ariseth . . . and this is the door of Gehenna."

Note what Ezra Abbott (Assistant Librarian of Harvard

College) wrote on this subject in Smith's *Bible Dictionary*, page 880:

> There is a remarkable passage in the book of Enoch which deserves notice here, as perhaps the earliest example in Jewish writings of the representation of Gehenna or the Valley of Hinnom as a place of punishment for the wicked . . . After the description, the passage continues thus: "Then I said: 'What means this blessed land which is full of trees, and this accursed valley in the midst?' Then Uriel, one of the holy angels with me, answered and said: 'This accursed valley is for those who shall be accursed to eternity: here must assemble all those who utter with their mouths unseemly speeches against God, and blaspheme his glory; here they are to be gathered, and this is the place of their punishment. And in the last times will the spectacle be given to the righteous of a just judgment on these for ever and ever; for which those who have found mercy will praise the Lord of glory, the eternal King.' " (See Isaiah 66:22-24.)

> "This," remarks a writer in the *National Review*, "is the earliest expression of the Jewish belief respecting the scene and mode of the Messianic crisis . . . The Judgement, it is plain, was to take place near Jerusalem: and while the temple hill was to be the citadel of reward to the pious, the punishment of the wicked, in order to be in sight, would take place in the Valley of Hinnom below. This spot, it is quite evident, is not figuratively referred to, as furnishing merely a name and symbol for the invisible penalties of another world, but literally designated as their royal topographical seat; precisely as the neighboring heights are taken to be the proper metropolis of the elect.

> Both physical and historical causes inclined the Jewish imagination to select this particular valley for the fatal purpose. Stretching towards the volcanic district to the South, it is said to have emitted at times a smoke which betrayed subterranean fires, and which put on the convulsions of the Asphaltite basin. And as the frequent

scene of the rites of Molech, it was associated with many
horrors, and had received the curse of the prophets."

On the subject of "The Valley of Hinnom," page 1078:

> From its ceremonial defilement, and from the detest-
> able and abominable fire of Molech, if not from the sup-
> posed everburning funeral piles, the later Jews applied
> the name of this Valley *Ge Hinnom, Gehenna,* to denote
> the place of eternal torment, and some of the Rabbins
> here fixed the "door of hell;" a sense in which it is used
> by our Lord.

Continuing this subject, read Matthew 10:28: "Be not
afraid of them that kill the body, but ARE NOT ABLE TO KILL
THE SOUL: but rather fear him who is able to destroy [APPO-
LUMI] both soul and body in GEHENNA." It is useless for a
Jehovah's Witness to argue that this proves extinction of the
soul, because this is the same Greek word used at Matthew
10:6 where Jesus instructed the apostles: "Go rather to the
lost [APPOLUMI] sheep of the house of Israel." Were these
"lost" sheep non-existent? Were they "destroyed" sheep? Of
course not! So the text, Matthew 10:28, shows that God can
cause our souls to be lost [APPOLUMI] in Gehenna—forever.

"Be not afraid of them that kill the body, and after that
have no more that they can do. But I will warn you whom
ye SHALL fear: Fear HIM, WHO AFTER HE HATH KILLED hath
power to CAST INTO GEHENNA; yea, I say unto you, FEAR HIM"
(Luke 12:4, 5).

Thayer's *Lexicon* on *Gehenna* gives the following:

> The valley of lamentation, or the sons of lamenta-
> tion . . . the name of a valley on the S. and E. of Jeru-
> salem, which was so called from the cries of the little
> children who were thrown into the fiery arms of Molech
> i.e., of an idol having the form of a bull. The Jews so
> abhorred the place after these horrible sacrifices had
> been abolished by King Josiah (2 Kings 23:10), that
> they cast into it not only all manner of refuse, but even
> the dead bodies of animals and of unburied criminals

who had been executed. And since fires were always needed to consume the dead bodies, that the air might not become tainted by the putrefaction, it came to pass that the place was called GEHENNA TOU PUROS [GEHENNA OF FIRE]; and then this name was transferred to that place in Hades where the wicked after death will suffer punishment.

But what about the Watchtower's idea that the story of the rich man and Lazarus is only a parable? Will that not lessen the argument in favor of eternal punishment? The historic Christian faith does not hold the account to be a parable. An excellent treatment of this subject is given by John Wesley. From *The Works of John Wesley,* Volume VII, page 245:

> But is the subsequent account merely a parable, or real history? It has been believed by many, and roundly asserted, to be a mere parable, because of one or two circumstances therein which are not easy to be accounted for. In particular, it is hard to conceive, how a person in hell could hold conversation with one in paradise. But, admitting we cannot account for this, will it overbalance an express assertion of our Lord: "There was," says our Lord, "a certain rich man."—Was there not? Did such a man never exist?
>
> "And there was a certain beggar named Lazarus." Was there, or was there not? Is it bold enough, positively to deny what our blessed Lord positively affirms? Therefore, we cannot reasonably doubt, but the whole narration, with all its circumstances, is exactly true. And Theophylact (one of the ancient commentators on the Scriptures) observes upon this text, that, "according to the tradition of the Jews, Lazarus lived at Jerusalem."

Next Wesley describes the entire account of the rich man and Lazarus as follows:

> First, I will endeavor, with God's assistance, to explain this history. "There was a certain rich man;" and, doubtless, on that very account, highly esteemed

among men,—"who was clothed in purple and fine linen;" and, consequently, esteemed the more highly, both as appearing suitably to his fortune, and as an encourager of trade;—"and fared sumptuously every day." Here was another reason for his being highly esteemed,—his hospitality and generosity,—both by those who frequently sat at his table, and the tradesmen that furnished it.

"And there was a certain beggar;" one in the lowest line of human infamy; "named Lazarus," according to the Greek termination; in Hebrew, Eleazer. From his name we may gather, that he was well known in the city, and it was a scandal to him to be named.—"Who was laid at his gate;" although no pleasing spectacle; so that one might wonder he was suffered to lie there;— "full of sores;" of running ulcers;—"and desiring to be fed with the crumbs which fell from the rich man's table." So the complicated affliction of poverty, pain, and want of bread, lay upon him at once! But it does not appear that any creature took the least notice of the despicable wretch! Only "the dogs came and licked his sores:" All the comfort which this world afforded him!

But see the change! "The beggar died:" Here ended poverty and pain:—"And was carried by angels:" nobler servants than any that attended the rich man;—"into Abraham's bosom:" So the Jews commonly termed what our blessed Lord styles paradise; the place "where the wicked cease from troubling, and where the weary are at rest:" But see the change again! "The rich man also died." What—must rich men also die? . . . "And was buried;" doubtless, with pomp enough, suitably to his quality. . . .

"And in hell he lifted up his eyes." O, what a change! How is the mighty fallen! But the word which is here rendered *hell* does not always mean the place of the damned. It is, literally, *the invisible world;* and it is of very wide extent, including the receptacle of separate spirits, whether good or bad. (Note: This does not necessarily mean, however, that the righteous and evil are together; see quotation from Smith's *Bible Diction-*

ary in this chapter.) "He seeth Abraham afar off." Far, indeed! as far as from hell to paradise! Perhaps, "tenfold the length of this terrene." But how could this be? I cannot tell: But it is by no means incredible. For who knows "how far an angel kens," or a spirit divested of flesh and blood?—"And Lazarus in his bosom."

It is well known that, in the ancient feasts among the Jews, as well as the Romans, the guests did not sit down at the table, as it is now the custom to do; but lay on couches, each having a pillow at his left side, on which he supported his elbow; and he that sat next to him, on the right side, was said to lie in his bosom. It was in this sense that the Apostle John lay in his Master's bosom. Accordingly, the expression of Lazarus lying in Abraham's bosom implies that he was in the highest place of honour and happiness.

"And he cried, and said, Father Abraham, have mercy on me."—Thou fool! What can Abraham do? What can can any creature, yes, all the creation do, to break the laws of the bottomless pit? Whoever would escape from the place of torment, let him cry to God, the Father of mercy! Nay, but the time is past! Justice now takes place, and rejoices over mercy!—"And send Lazarus, that he may dip the tip of his finger in water, and cool my tongue; for I am tormented in this flame!"

"How exceeding modest a request is this! He does not say, "That he may take me out of this flame." He does not ask, "That he may bring me a cup of water, or as much as he might hold in the palm of his hand;" but barely, "That he may dip" were it but "the tip of his finger in water, and cool my tongue." No! It cannot be! No mercy can enter within the shades of hell!

But Abraham said, "Son, remember that thou in thy lifetime receivedst thy good things, and likewise Lazarus evil things; but now he is comforted, and thou tormented." Perhaps these words may supply us with an answer to an important question: How came this rich man to be in hell? It does not appear that he was a wicked man, in the common sense of the word; that he was a drunkard, a common swearer, a Sabbath-breaker, or that he lived in any known sin. It is probable he was a Pharisee; and as such was, in all the outward parts of religion, blameless.

How then did he come into "the place of torment?" If there was no other reason to be assigned, there is a sufficient one implied in those words, "Thou in thy lifetime receivedst thy good things;" the things which thou hadst chosen for thy happiness. Thou didst receive the portion which thou hadst chosen, and canst have no portion above. "And likewise Lazarus evil things." Not *his* evil things; for he did not choose them. But they were chosen for him by the wise providence of God: And "now he is comforted, while thou art tormented."

"But, besides all this, there is a great gulf fixed:" A great chasm, a vast vacuity. Can any tell us what this is? What is the nature, what are the bounds, of it? Nay, none of the children of men; none but an inhabitant of the invisible world.—"So that they who would pass from hence to you cannot; neither can they pass to us, that would come from thence." Undoubtedly a disembodied spirit could pass through any space whatsoever. But the will of God, determining that none should go across the gulf, is a bound which no creature can pass.

Then he said, "I pray thee therefore, father, that thou wouldst send him to my father's house; for I have five brethren, that he may testify unto them, lest they come also into this place of torment." Two entirely different motives have been assigned for this extraordinary request. Some ascribe it wholly to self love, to a fear of the bitter reproaches which, he might easily suppose, his brethren would pour upon him, if, in consequence of his example, and perhaps advice, they came to the same place of torment.

Others have imputed it to a nobler motive. They suppose, as the misery of the wicked will not be complete till the day of judgment, so neither will their wickedness. Consequently, they believe that, all that time, they may retain some sparks of mutual affection; and they, not improbably, imagine that this may have occasioned his desire to prevent their sharing his own torment.

"Abraham saith unto him, They have Moses and the Prophets; let them hear them." "And he said, Nay, father Abraham; but if one went to them from the dead, they will repent." Who would not be of the same opinion? Might not any one reasonably suppose that a message solemnly delivered by one that came from the dead must have an irresistible force? Who would not think, "I myself could not possibly withstand such a preacher of righteousness?" This I conceive to be the meaning of the words. I will now endeavor, with the help of God, to apply them.

It is no more sinful to be rich than to be poor. But it is dangerous beyond expression. Therefore, I remind all of you that are of this number, that have the conveniences of life, and something over, that ye walk upon slippery ground. Ye are every moment on the verge of hell! "It is easier for a camel to go through the eye of a needle, than for you to enter into the kingdom of heaven." . . . Whoever thou art that sharest in the sin of this rich man, were it no other than 'faring sumptuously every day,' thou shalt as surely be a sharer in his punishment, except thou repent, as if thou wert already crying for a drop of water to cool thy tongue!

"And he cried, and said, Father Abraham, have mercy upon me!"—I do not remember, in all the Bible, any prayer made to a saint, but this. And if we observe who made it,—a man in hell,—and with what success, we shall hardly wish to follow the precedent . . . You are not past the great gulf, but have it still in your power to choose whether you will be attended by angels or fiends when your soul quits its earthly mansion.

Now stretch out your hand to eternal life or eternal death!

. . . He makes another request: "I pray thee, send him to my father's house; for I have five brethren; that he may testify to them." It is not impossible that other unhappy spirits may wish well to the relations they have left behind them . . . We are indeed apt to think, like that unhappy spirit, "If one went to them from the dead, they will repent. But Abraham said, If they hear not

Moses and the Prophets, neither will they be persuaded though one rose from the dead."

It is certain that no human spirit, while it is in the body, can *persuade* another *to repent;* can work in him an entire change, both of heart and life; a change from universal wickedness, to universal holiness. And suppose that spirit discharged from the body, it is no more able to do this than it was before. No power less than that which created it first can create any soul anew. . . .

No angel, much less any human spirit, whether in the body or out of the body, can bring one soul "from darkness to light, and from the power of Satan unto God." It might very possibly fright him to death, or to the belief of any speculative truth; but it could not frighten him unto spiritual life.

Several quotations from Hastings' *Dictionary of the Bible* will prove valuable. The first is on *Hell,* Volume II, page 343:

> The term used in Old English to designate the world of the dead generally with all the sad and painful associations of the dark region into which the living disappear. In modern English it has the specific sense of the place and condition of penalty destined for the finally impenitent among the dead. With this it expresses also the abode of evil spirits.

The same volume under *Gehenna,* page 119:

> It signifies the *place of punishment for rebellious or apostate Jews in the presence of the righteous. Gehinnom* or *Gehenna* is not actually mentioned with this signification in the OT, but it is it and no other place that is implied in Isa. 50:11 "in a place of pain shall ye lie down," and 66:24 with this new connotation.
>
> Further, the punishment of the apostate Jews in Isa. 66:24 is conceived as eternal: "They shall look upon the carcasses of the men that have transgressed against me; for their worm shall not die, neither shall their fire be quenched, and they shall be an abhorring to all

flesh." The punishment of Gehenna is implied in Dan. 12:2, 'some to shame and everlasting *abhorrence*' which occurs in these two passages, and in these only, and the reference in both is to *Gehenna*.

On page 344, again under *Gehenna:*

The terrible associations of the place, the recollections of the horrors perpetrated in it and the defilement inflicted on it, the fires said to have been kept burning in it in order to consume the foul and corrupt objects that were thrown into it, made it a natural and unmistakable symbol of dire evil torment, wasting penalty, absolute ruin. So it came to designate the place of future punishment, and the Talmudic theology spoke of the door of hell as being in the valley of Hinnom.

Page 345:

In the theology of the Talmud and Midrash, *Gehinnom, Gehenna* meant the scene of penalty, while in certain phases of Jewish belief it appears to have been regarded at once as a place of punishment for the heathen and as a place of purgatorial detention for imperfect Israelites. But with all this there is reason to say its original sense was that of the final place of retribution, that it was distinguished from *Hades* and from every form of an intermediate state, and that it had this meaning with the Jewish people generally in Christ's time.

The apocalyptic writings, which speak of a separation of the just from the unjust between death and the resurrection, also speak of a final punishment after the judgment, and describe the place of that retribution in terms which point to Gehenna.

Matthew 18:8 warns:

And if thy hand or thy foot causeth thee to stumble, cut it off, and cast it from thee: it is good for thee to enter life maimed or halt [Jehovah's Witnesses scoff and ridicule this], rather than having two hands or two feet to be CAST INTO THE ETERNAL FIRE [TO PUR TO AIONION].

Revelation 14:9-11:

> If any man worshipeth the beast and his image, and
> receiveth a mark on his forehead, or upon his hand, he
> shall also drink of the wine of the wrath of God, which
> is prepared unmixed in the cup of his anger; and he
> shall be tormented *(basanizo)* with fire and brimstone in
> the presence of the holy angels and in the presence of
> the Lamb; and the smoke of their torment *(basanismos)*
> goeth up for ever and ever.

The *Schaff-Herzog Encyclopedia* regarding *Gehenna* (Volume IV, page 443) :

> Thus it became customary to call the place of punish-
> ment of the Jewish wicked "valley of Hinnom." The
> name was retained after the idea of the place of punish-
> ment in the last day had severed itself from that locality
> and its connotation expanded to mean the place of
> punishment for all men . . . The place of everlasting
> punishment after the last judgment was located by the
> Pharisees under the earth. . . . It is placed in opposition
> to the "dominion of God" or "eternal life" and denotes
> the state which falls to the final lot of the ungodly, and
> this, according to Matt. 10:28, affects both soul and
> body.

Volume V, page 109 concerning *Hades:*

> The Israelitic conception of Sheol rests upon the
> belief that the decomposition of the dead body, by
> means of which dust returns to dust, does not involve
> complete annihilation, only that in death the "shade" of
> the living man separates from the body and takes up its
> abode in Sheol.

Jehovah's Witnesses will argue (in spite of what the Scriptures say) that Jehovah is only a God of love, and would
never send anyone to the kind of Hell *we* describe! They are
not acquainted with the *real* Jehovah, but only a *Watchtower
Jehovah,* a figment of their imagination! Jehovah said to
Moses: "I will be gracious to whom I will be gracious, and

will show mercy on whom I will show mercy" (Exodus 33: 19). The New Testament quotes this at Romans 9:15.

Speaking of believers, Paul said at Ephesians 1:5: "Having foreordained (PROORIZO, determined before, predestinated) us unto adoption as sons through Jesus Christ unto himself, according to the good pleasure of HIS WILL." Here we see that it is GOD'S WILL (not ours) in action here. Verse 11 from the King James Version: "In whom also we have obtained an inheritance, being predestinated according to the purpose of him who worketh all things after the counsel of HIS OWN WILL."

In Paul's writings we learn much about the ways of Jehovah. The Jehovah's Witnesses (who are certainly misnamed!) criticize God for being the kind of God the Bible says He is. Read Romans 9:16, 18-23 regarding this:

> So then it is NOT OF HIM THAT WILLETH, nor of him that runneth, BUT OF GOD that hath mercy. . . . So then he hath mercy ON WHOM HE WILL, and who he will he hardeneth (SKLERUNO). Thou wilt say then unto me, Why doth he still find fault? [That is to say, Why does He find fault with us if he made us the way we are?] Nay but, O man, who art thou that repliest against God? Shall the thing formed say to him that formed it, Why didst thou make me thus? Or hath not the potter A RIGHT OVER THE CLAY, from the same lump to make ONE PART A VESSEL UNTO HONOR, AND ANOTHER UNTO DISHONOR?
>
> What if God, although willing to show his wrath, and to make his power known, endured with much longsuffering vessels of wrath fitted unto destruction: that he might make known THE RICHES OF HIS GLORY UPON VESSELS OF MERCY, WHICH HE AFORE PREPARED [PROETOMAZO] UNTO GLORY.

What is the *opposite* of "a vessel of mercy?" A *reprobate*. Read II Corinthians 13:5: "Try your own selves, whether ye are in the faith; prove your own selves. Or know ye not as to your own selves, that Jesus is in you? Unless indeed ye be reprobate."

Indeed, Jehovah's Witnesses know nothing at all about *this* Jehovah! ALL is under His authoritative rule and decree, whether we care to admit it or not. Before any rage in protest against Jehovah for what He is, see His words, Isaiah 45:9: "Woe unto him that striveth with his Maker! a potsherd among the potsherds of the earth! Shall the clay say to him that fashioneth it, What makest thou?" We had better learn who and what God is and keep silent before Him after we do so.

Commenting, Matthew Henry's *Commentary* says, Volume IV, page 253:

> For reproof to those of the church's enemies that opposed this salvation, or those of her friends that despaired of it: *Woe unto him that strives with his Maker!* God is the Maker of all things, and therefore our Maker, which is the reason why we should always submit to him and never contend with him.

> Sinful man is indeed a quarrelsome creature; but *let the potsherds strive with the potsherds of the earth.* Men are but earthen pots, nay, they are broken potsherds, and are so very much by their mutual contentions. They are dashed in pieces one against another; and if they are disposed to strive, let them strive with one another, let them meddle with their match; but let them not dare to contend with him that is infinitely above them, which is as senseless and absurd as for the clay to find fault with the potter: Shall the clay say to him that forms it, *"What makest thou?* Why dost thou make me of this shape and not that?"

> Nay, it is as if the clay should be in such a heat and passion with the potter as to tell him that *he has no hands,* or that he works as awkwardly as if he had none. "Shall the clay pretend to be wiser than the potter and therefore control him?" He that gave us being, that gave us this being, may design concerning us, and DISPOSE OF

US AS HE PLEASES; and it is impudent presumption for us to prescribe to him. [Emphasis mine.]

Shall we impeach God's wisdom, or question his power, who are ourselves so curiously, so wonderfully made? Shall we say, He has no hands, whose made us and in whose hands we are? The doctrine of God's sovereignty has enough in it to silence all our discontents and objections against the methods of his providence and grace, (Romans 9:20, 21). It is as unnatural for the child to find fault with the parents, to say to the father, *"What begettest thou?"* or the mother, *"What has thou brought forth?"* Why was I not begotten and born an angel, exempt from the infirmities of human nature and the calamities of human life?" Must not those who are children of men expect to share in the common lot and fare as others fare? If God is our Father, where is the honor we owe to him by submitting to his will?

Opposers will use another example to make it appear as if we can pit our will against that of Almighty God. They believe that doing so we will prove to be His match. They quote the *King James Version of Psalm* 78:41, "Yea, they turned back and tempted God, and LIMITED the Holy One of Israel."

Here are some *other* translations:

Yea, they turned back, and tempted God, and PROVOKED the Holy One of Israel (Bagster's *Septuagint*).

They actually turned back and tempted God, and PROVOKED TO WRATH the Holy One of Israel (Thomason's *Septuagint*).

And they turned again and tempted God, and PROVOKED the Holy One of Israel (ASV).

With doubts of God again and again, that PAINED the Majestic One of Israel (Moffat).

Yea, again and again they tempted God, and the Holy One of Israel they VEXED (*Expositor's Bible*).

Always new challenges to God's power, NEW REBELLIONS against the Holy One of Israel" (Ronald Knox).

It is only bigoted, egotistical men who think they can

thwart the will of Almighty God. No one has ever limited the Holy One of Israel and no one ever will!

We read of the sad end of sinful men, unborn by the Spirit:

> Depart from me under a curse, INTO THE ETERNAL FIRE [TO PUR TO AIONION] which is prepared for the devil and his angels (Matthew 25:41).

> So shall it be in the consummation of the age: the angels shall come forth, and sever the wicked from among the righteous, and shall cast them into the FURNACE OF FIRE [TEN KAMINON TOU PUROS]: there shall be the weeping and the gnashing of teeth (Matthew 13:49, 50).

> Jude 7 reads: Even as Sodom and Gomorrah, and the cities about them, having in like manner with these given themselves over to fornication and gone after strange flesh, are set forth as AN EXAMPLE OF ETERNAL FIRE, suffering PUNISHMENT OF ETERNAL FIRE.

The *Let God Be True* book says, in its typical childish fashion, page 93:

> But are not Satan the Devil and his demons down in hell keeping the fires and making it hard for those who are in it? That is what is taught by Christendom's clergy, but you will be surprised to know the Devil never was in such a place. The Devil's human servant, the king of Babylon, was doomed to go to hell, the Bible hell. But Satan the Devil who made himself Lucifer in his organization is really the one spoken to under the figure of "the king of Babylon" in these words. "Hell from beneath is moved for thee, at thy coming: it stirreth up the dead for thee, even all the chief ones of the earth; it hath raised up from their thrones all the kings of the nations" (Isaiah 14:9). If the Devil had been there constantly, how could hell be moved to meet him?

Without a shred of evidence to confirm their statements, the Watchtower Society leads the Witnesses along, like animals to the slaughter. The above is typical of material contained in *Let God Be True*. The Witnesses will believe what the Society tells them, because they fear the New World organization.

Is there a *human* "king of Babylon" only? It is true that Satan is spoken to in Isaiah 14 under the figure of the king of Babylon. But in recognizing this, let us not ignore the king who literally sat upon the throne. What does Isaiah say of him? Matthew Henry's *Commentary,* Vol. IV, page 86:

> The king of Babylon, having so much wealth in his dominions and the absolute command of it, by the help of that *ruled the nations* (v. 6), gave them law, read them their doom, and at his pleasure *weakened the nations* (v. 12), that they might not be able to make head against him. Such vast and victorious armies did he bring into the field, that, which soever way he looked, he *made the earth to tremble, and shook kingdoms,* (v. 16); all his neighbors were afraid of him, and were forced to submit to him. No man could do this by his own personal strength, but by the numbers he had at his back. Great tyrants, by making some do what they will, make others suffer what they will. How piteous is the case of mankind, which thus seems to be in a combination against itself, and its own rights and liberties, which could not be ruined but by its own strength!
>
> The wretched abuse of all this wealth and power, which the king of Babylon was guilty of, in two instances:— (1.) Great oppression and cruelty. He is known by the name *oppressor* (v. 4). He has the *sceptre of the rulers* (v. 5), has the command of all the princes about him; but it is *the staff of the wicked,* a staff with which he supports himself in his wickedness and wickedly strikes all about him. *He smote the people,* not in justice, for their correction and reformation, but *in wrath* (v. 6), to gratify his own peevish resentment, and that *with a continual stroke,* pursued them with his forces, and gave them no respite, no breathing time, no cessation of arms.
>
> He ruled the nations, but he ruled them *in anger,* everything he said and did was in a passion; so that he

who had the government all about him, had no government of himself. He *made the world as a wilderness,* as if he had taken pride in being the plague of his generation and a curse to mankind, v. 17. Great princes usually glory in building cities, but he gloried in destroying them; see Psalms 9:6. Two particular instances, worse than all the rest, are here given of his tyranny:

(1.) That he was severe to his captives (v. 17): He *opened not the house of his prisoners;* he *did not let them loose homeward* (so the marginal reads it); he kept them in close confinement, and never would suffer any to return to their own land . . . . (2.) That he was oppressive to his own subjects (v. 20): *Thou hast destroyed thy land, and slain thy people;* and what did he get by that, when the wealth of the land and the multitude of the people are the strength and honour of the prince, who never rules so safely, so gloriously, as in the hearts of the people?

(2.) Great pride and haughtiness. Notice is here taken of his *pomp,* the extravagancy of his retinue, v. 11. He affected to appear in the utmost significance. But that was not the worst: It was the temper of his mind, and the elevation of that, that ripened him for ruin (v. 13, 14); *Thou hast said in thy heart* (like Lucifer), *I will ascend into heaven.* Here is the language of his vain glory, borrowed perhaps from that of the angels who fell, who not content with their first estate, the post assigned them, would vie with God, and become not only independent of Him, but equal with Him. Or perhaps it refers to the story of Nebuchadnezzar, who, when he would be more than a man, was justly turned into a brute (Dan. 4:30).

The king of Babylon promises himself, (1.) That in pomp and power he shall surpass all his neighbors . . . . (2.) That he shall particularly insult over God's Mount Zion, which Belshazzar, in his last drunken frolic, seems to have had a particular spite against when he called for the vessels of the temple at Jerusalem, to profane them; see Daniel 5:2. In the same humour he here said, *I will sit upon the mount of the congregation* (it is the same word that is used for the holy *convocations*), *in the sides of the north;* so Mount Zion is said to be situated, Psalms 48:2 . . . .

(3) That he shall vie with the God of Israel, of whom he had indeed heard glorious things, that he had his residence *above the heights of the clouds.* "But thither," says he, *"I will ascend,* and be as great as he; I will be like him whom they call *the Most High."*

(4) That she shall himself be deified after his death, as some of the first founders of the Assyrian monarchy were, and stars had even their names from them. "But," says he, *"I will exalt my throne above them all."*

3. The utter ruin that should be brought upon him. It is foretold, (1.) That his wealth and power should be broken, and a final period put to his pomp and pleasure . . . . (2.) That he himself should be seized . . . . (3.) That he should be slain, and *go down to the congregation of the dead* . . . His *pomp is brought down to the grave* (v. 11) , that is, it perishes with him. . . .

4. The many triumphs that should be in his fall. (1.) Those whom he had been a great tyrant and terror to will be glad they are rid of him (v. 7, 8) . (2.) The congregation of the dead will bid him welcome to them, especially those whom he had barbarously hastened thither (v. 9, 10) . *"Hell from beneath is moved for thee, to meet thee at thy coming,* and to compliment thee upon thy arrival at their dark and dreadful regions." *The chief ones of the earth,* who when they were alive were kept in awe by him and durst not come near him, but rose from their thrones to resign them to him, shall upbraid him with it when he comes into the state of the dead.

They shall go forth to meet him, as they used to do when he made his public entry into cities he had become master of; with such a parade he shall be introduced into these regions of horror, to make his disgrace the more grievous to him. They shall scoffingly rise from their thrones and seats there, and ask him if he will please to sit down with them, as he used to do in their thrones on earth?

The confusion that will then cover him they shall

make a jest of: "Hast thou also become as weak as we?"
Who would have thought it? It is what thou thyself
didst not expect it would ever come to when thou wast
in everything too hard for us. Thou that didst then rank
thyself among the immortal gods, art thou come to take
thy fate among us poor mortal men? Where is thy pomp
now, and where is thy mirth?

Now this reception of the king of Babylon into the
regions of the dead, which is here described, surely is
something more than a flight of fancy, and is designed
to teach these solid truths:— (1.) That there is an invisible world, a world of spirits, to which the souls of
men remove at death and in which they exist and act in
a state of separation from the body. (2.) That separate souls have acquaintance and converse with each
other, though we have none with them. . . . (3.) That
death and hell will be death and hell indeed to those
of this world's pomps and the fulness of its pleasures.

In its typical fashion the *Let God Be True* book pro-
nounces this erroneous decree on page 97:

After Jesus pronounced judgment on the "goats," who
do not support God's kingdom to which Christ's broth-
ers are called, he declares respecting the "goats:" "These
will depart into everlasting cutting-off (Greek, *kolasis*),
but the righteous ones into everlasting life." (Matthew
25:46, *NW ED*) So the everlasting punishment of the
"goats" is their everlastingly being cut off from all life.

However, at I John 4:18 the *New World* translation itself
translates the Greek word KOLASIS as "restraint, correction,
punishment," and *The Emphatic Diaglott* renders Matthew
25:46: "And these shall go forth to the aionian cutting-off,"
with footnote: "THAT IS, IN THE FIRE MENTIONED IN VERSE 41."

Let God Be True on page 91 poses the problem as to
where Hell is. They use the case of Jonah in the fish (or
whale) to try and prove *their* theory of where Hell is. They
quote Jonah 2:1, 2: "Then Jonah prayed unto Jehovah his
God out of the fish's belly. And he said, I called out of mine

affliction unto Jehovah, and he answered me; Out of the belly of Sheol cried I, and thou heardest my voice."

They conclude from this that the fish's belly became Jonah's *Sheol*. But here is what they do not know: The Bible shows that Jonah prayed two times, from two *different* places! First, he prayed from the belly (Hebrew, BETEN) of Sheol. This word also carries the translation *womb*. Then he prayed from the fish's belly (Hebrew, MEIM). Here is how Charles Thomson's translation of the *Septuagint* reads at this verse: "And from out of the belly of the great whale, Jonas prayed to the Lord his God, and said: In my affliction I cried [past tense] to the Lord my God, and He hearkened [*past* tense] to me. Thou didst hear [*past* tense] my cry from the womb of Hades, Thou didst hearken [*past* tense] to my prayer."

Note: Jonah *first* prayed from the depths of the sea (2:3, 5-7) and was heard, and Jehovah delivered him from drowning by having the fish swallow him. It was after three days and three nights there (1:17) that Jonah then prayed again (2:1), following which Jehovah had the fish vomit him out upon the dry land (2:10).

In this poetic chapter Jonah parallels his deliverance from imminent death in the sea's depths to a removal from *Sheol* itself. Not that the two are identical, but that they are similar in many ways. Notice verse 4: "And I said, I am cast out from before thy eyes." Jonah had willfully withdrawn from standing in God's presence. Now God had taken him at his word, and, as it seemed, cast him out of it.

This idea of being expelled from God's presence—which is truly the state of the souls dwelling in *Sheol*—is what caused Jonah to liken the depths of the sea (v. 5) to the abode of the wicked dead (v. 2). Furthermore, he knew that he was there "forever" (v. 6), so far as his own power of deliverance was concerned—another fact true also of *Sheol*. And even as he was alive and conscious when in his *Sheol*-like condition, so are those who have entered into the true *Sheol*. They are no more extinct than Jonah was! And for them, Christ has revealed (Luke 16:19-31), there is no escape. This then, and not the fish's belly or the sea, is the true *Sheol*. Discern carefully lest you be found believing every oracle sent forth by *The Watchtower Society*. Consider:

"It is so plain that the Bible hell is mankind's common grave that even an honest little child can understand it, but not the religious theologians." (*Let God Be True*, page 92.) They *must* say this in order to keep the Witnesses away from real theological investigation. They have to make it appear a sin to conduct an honest (and thorough) investigation into the Scriptures. What they really mean in the above quotation is that a child who is easily led and who is uneducated can be easily deceived. One who is not mature enough to think out theological matters for himself wants or needs someone else to think for him. This encourages some adults with dependent minds to remain immature.

If *Watchtower* is the truth and is so easy to understand, why is there such an array of Scripture against it? Why do they have such difficulty in making known this "truth?" Why the necessity of rewriting parts of the Bible? Yes—why the necessity of ADDING TO the Bible? Why the denial of almost every doctrine of the original historic Christian faith? Why the repudiation of almost everything Christians have held since the days when Jesus was here?

Paul says: "As we have said before, so say I now again, If any man preacheth unto you ANY GOSPEL CONTRARY TO THAT WHICH YE RECEIVED, let him be anathema" (Galatians 1:9).

Here is an example of the typical *Watchtower* method of wresting the Scriptures, by quoting OUT OF CONTEXT and then building heresy upon it. In Ezekiel 18:20, one of their favorite texts, quoted out of context: "The soul that sinneth, it shall die," then the Jehovah's Witness shuts his Bible, for that is as far as he cares to go!

For our answer to him we just read on. Verse 21 reads: "BUT IF the wicked will TURN FROM all his sins that he hath committed, and keep all my statutes, and DO THAT WHICH IS LAWFUL AND RIGHT, he shall surely LIVE, HE SHALL NOT DIE."

Yet, those who believed and turned to God (including Ezekiel), to whom this verse was written, died! And God here promised that they *would not* die! Applying this text Watchtower-fashion, God was a liar. Either that or the Watchtower is lying. Two contradictory teachings cannot both be true.

Evidently God was not speaking about physical death when he said the sinning soul would die. Both believers and unbelievers die physically. Certainly Ezekiel turned from his sins; yet he died! We read in verses 27 and 28:

> When the wicked man turneth away from his wickedness that he hath committed, and doeth that which is lawful and right, he shall save his soul alive. Because he considereth, and turneth away from all his transgressions, he shall save his soul alive. Because he considereth, and turneth away from all his transgressions that he hath committed, he shall surely live, HE SHALL NOT DIE.

But they died!

You see, this is speaking about a death that Jehovah's Witnesses know nothing about. It is speaking about SPIRITUAL DEATH OF THE SOUL. This is the condition of those who are lost and who shall be turned into Hell. The scoffers will scoff no more when turned into that place. Jehovah's Witnesses raise an objection to this doctrine. They do not understand passages like Revelation 20:14: "And death and Hades were cast into the lake of fire. This is the second death, the lake of fire."

Hades is *not* the "lake of fire." *That* is *Gehenna*. Those in Hades awaiting the final judgment are like those in death row in prison. They have already been sentenced, but the sentence will not be carried out until the order for execution arrives. There is a date set, and the execution order arrives at that time. On judgment day the awful words will be spoken: "Depart from me, ye cursed, into the ETERNAL FIRE which is prepared for the devil and his angels" (Matthew 25:41).

In *Harper's Bible Dictionary* on the subject:

> From being merely the shadowy abode of departed
> spirits the conception of hell was elaborated until it
> stood for a place of unspeakable terrors, especially in
> the so-called Apocalyptic Literature, of which the Reve-
> lation of St. John is the chief example in the N. T. The
> concept occurs in some of the sayings of Jesus (Matt.
> 5:29; 23:33), and in several of his parables (Matt. 25);
> and it is implied in such teachings as John 3:16-18, 36;
> 15:6.

Same dictionary, under *Everlasting Punishment:*

> He (Jesus) has freed a man from an evil spirit. His
> critics, observing the deed, declared that he could "cast
> out demons" because he was himself in league with "the
> prince of demons." Jesus took this to mean that they
> were morally blind—so committed to their own ideas
> that they could look on a deed which judged by any
> standard should be esteemed good, and say that it was
> evil and wrought by an evil power.

> He said that men who talked like this were doing far
> worse than defaming him: they were blaspheming the
> Holy Spirit by whom eventually every good deed was
> done. He implied that they had become so hardened
> that they could no longer respond to the appeal of the
> good. In that case they could never repent, and if they
> could not repent God could not forgive them. They
> were, in a word, so impervious to the Holy Spirit that
> they were beyond redemption.

> This incident shows the true meaning of everlasting
> punishment. In sharp contrast stands the idea of eter-
> nal life. The emphasis in the phrase "eternal life" is
> not on *time* but on *worth*. . . . Sometimes the contrast
> is between having eternal life and "perishing," as in the
> familiar John 3:16. To "perish" DOES NOT MEAN TO
> CEASE TO EXIST; it means failure to come to that TRUE
> LIFE which God intended every man to find. Final fail-
> ure will come to no man except of his own will; it will

bc thc rcsult of his refusal to accept eternal life. His
continuance in existence will be continuence in "death"
(the absence of true life) in a future life as much as in
this world. (Emphasis mine.)

Said the Psalmist: "Though I walk THROUGH the valley
(Hebrew, *gay,* a low plain or gorge) of the deep darkness of
DEATH, I will fear no evil; FOR THOU ART WITH ME" (Psalm
23:4). "In thy land of peace hast thou been secure? how wilt
thou act at the swelling of the Jordan?" (Jeremiah 12:5,
Thomson). When you must finally stand at the portals of
death, what will your actions be? Will there be someone to
guide you through the valley and over Jordan's chilly waters
to the other side? Or will you face those cold, dark waters all
alone? The judgment you must also face—all alone—for it is
your trial!

Consider these words, John 3:26, *Amplified New Testament:*

> And he who believes on—has faith in, clings to, relies
> on—the Son has (now possesses) eternal life. But who-
> ever disobeys—is unbelieving toward, refuses to trust in,
> disregards, is not subject to—the Son will never see (ex-
> perience) life. But instead the wrath of God abides
> on him—God's displeasure remains on him; His indigna-
> tion hangs over him continually. (Hab. 2:4).

There is no need for you to fear, *if* you would be *saved.*
"If a man keep my word, HE SHALL NEVER SEE DEATH" said
Jesus (John 8:51). What is your reaction to this invitation?
When Jesus spoke on these matters the Jews accused Him of
being demonized. They said: "Now we know that thou hast
a demon!" He had promised them that they would never die
if they would believe! It is the very same accusation that
Jehovah's Witnesses level today against Christians who hold
to this truth that Jesus taught.

You may be free forever from fear of eternal punishment,
for Jesus said: "My sheep hear my voice, and I know them,

and they follow me: and I GIVE UNTO THEM ETERNAL LIFE, and they shall NEVER PERISH" (John 10:27, 28). Further on: "I am the resurrection and the life: he that believeth on me, THOUGH HE DIE, YET SHALL HE LIVE; and whosoever liveth and BELIEVETH ON ME SHALL NEVER DIE" (John 11:25, 26). Thus he shows us the difference between physical and spiritual death. Though a Christian dies physically, he lives on spiritually.

The Watchtower Society insists that Satan challenged Jehovah's supremacy and that an issue was raised over who was supreme. They claim that Satan said to Jehovah that He could not put someone on earth who would remain faithful amid trials unto death. They say Jesus proved that Satan was wrong by doing all this. They call this the issue of "Universal Sovereignty." The Bible does not teach this, but they believe it anyway. To them Armageddon (Revelation 16:16) will "prove" that Jehovah is supreme by destroying all non-Jehovah's Witnesses.

However, with all thanks to God, the redeemed can now say: "NOT BY WORKS done in righteousness, which WE DID OURSELVES, but according to MERCY he saved us, through the WASHING OF REGENERATION and through RENEWING OF THE HOLY SPIRIT" (Titus 3:5). You can be delivered NOW!

"And one said unto him, Lord, are they few that are saved? And he said unto them, Strive to enter in by the narrow door: for many, I say unto you, shall seek to enter in, and shall not be able" (Luke 13:23, 24). This is what you must face: PRESENT SALVATION OR ETERNAL PUNISHMENT. Consider what is offered: "I am the door; by me if any man enter [*present* tense] in, HE SHALL BE SAVED (John 10:9). Paul, writing to the Romans, says: "But God commendeth HIS OWN LOVE TOWARD US, in that, WHILE WE WERE YET SINNERS, Christ died for us. Much more then, being now JUSTIFIED IN HIS BLOOD, shall we be SAVED FROM THE WRATH OF GOD THROUGH HIM" (Romans 5:8, 9).

"If thou shalt confess with thy mouth JESUS as Lord, and shalt BELIEVE in thy heart that God raised him from the dead,

THOU SHALT BE SAVED" (Romans 10:9). "For by GRACE have ye been saved through FAITH; and that NOT OF YOURSELVES, it is the GIFT OF GOD: NOT OF WORKS, that no man should glory" (Ephesians 2:8, 9). You must accept it free or not at all. Again, if you reject the Gospel there is no need to await an Armageddon to know your fate: "He that believeth not IS JUDGED ALREADY" (John 3:18).

It is the writer's desire that at this moment that you (if you are unsaved) will yield your all to the Saviour. You may come to Christ on the basis of the faith you have at this moment. To all who will do so: "Ye are of God, my little children, and have overcome [the Spirit of anti-Christ]: because greater is he that is in you than he that is in the world" (I John 4:4).

"Now unto him that is able to guard you from stumbling, and to set you before the presence of his glory without blemish in exceeding joy, to the only God our Saviour, through Jesus Christ our Lord, be glory, majesty, dominion and power, before all time, and now, and for evermore. Amen" (Jude 24, 25).

"The grace of the Lord Jesus Christ be with your spirit" (Philippians 4:23).

Chapter Six

THE SECOND COMING OF
THE SON OF GOD

SINCE THE WATCHTOWER system has so thoroughly altered the truth about the first Advent of Jesus Christ, we can rightly expect them to do the same with the second Advent. Using false reasoning rather than Scripture, they arrive at a far-fetched idea, using some clever mathematics taken from the Scriptures (wrongfully).

In Hebrews 9:28 we are told: "Christ also, having been once offered to bear the sins of many, shall appear a second time, to them that wait for him, unto salvation." Acts 1:11 reads: "This Jesus, who was received up from you into heaven, shall so come in like manner as ye beheld him going into heaven."

The Watchtower cries out its opposition to this in *Let God Be True,* page 196: "Jesus Christ returns, not again as a human, but as a glorious spirit person." On page 198, under *How Seen:* "His return is recognized by the eyes of one's understanding, such eyes being enlightened by God's unfolding Word."

They then bring into question the Greek word PAROUSIA. Here is what they say about it on page 198: "The meaning of *parousia* is more exact than the word 'coming' contained in the general English versions. It does not mean he is on the way or has promised to come, but that he has already arrived and is here." Page 199 states: "It is not necessary for Christ to be visible at his presence, even as his Father is not visible to human sight. . . . Today the evidence of Christ's presence is all about us, and yet so-called 'Christendom' does not see it."

The Witnesses think that an invisible "presence" of the Lord has already taken place! *Let God Be True* states on page 201: "For many years prior to 1914 earnest Bible students (Russellites) understood that the year 1914 marked the end of the Gentile times or the 'appointed times of the nations.' That date marked the beginning of the 'time of the end' of Satan's rule, and therefore the time when Christ Jesus the righteous Ruler of the new world received control."

What do they think happened in 1914? Page 203 explains: "The dead Christians sleeping in the graves were raised with spirit bodies to join him at the spiritual temple. . . . Returning after a long time, he judges his slaves. To the faithful he gives greater privileges and the joy of their Master. The unfaithful (all non-Jehovah's Witnesses) are thrown into the darkness outside the theocratic organization."

On this same subject we go to page 205 and read these words: "The final revelation of the King draws nearer. The disaster of Armageddon, greater than that which befell Sodom and Gomorrah, is at the door. . . . The nearness of that event is causing the selfish ones to band together and hide themselves in human organizations for protection." The fact that Jehovah's Witnesses are hiding within an organization seems to escape their notice!

Continuing on to page 206: "Christ returns before his thousand-year undisturbed reign to put all enemies under his feet at Armageddon. . . . By clearing out false religion (all faiths except their own), by restoring true worship (forced rule of the *New World Society*), and by re-establishing the divine government toward our earth, he reveals his kingly power of which he proved himself worthy at his first coming."

Before going further, we should give attention to the fact that much is made over the Greek word PAROUSIA. Most of the Witnesses do not know the slightest thing about Greek and therefore have not the faintest idea as to the real meaning of the word. They only know what the Watchtower Society tells them. Thayer's *Greek Lexicon* says regarding this word: "The presence of one coming, hence the *coming, arrival, ad-*

vent. . . . In the N. T. especially of *the advent* i.e., the future, visible *return* from heaven of Jesus, the Messiah, to raise the dead, hold the last judgment, and set up formally and gloriously the kingdom of God."

However, PAROUSIA is not the only word in the Greek Scriptures used regarding Christ's second Advent. Consider the word APOKALUPSIS for example. It is used at I Peter 1:7: "That the proof of your faith, being more precious than gold that perisheth though it is proved by the fire, may be found unto praise and glory and honor at the revelation (APOKA-LUPSIS) of Jesus Christ." Again in I Corinthians 1:7 we find these words: "Waiting for the revelation (APOKALUPSIS) of our Lord Jesus Christ."

Bullinger's lexicon defines this word APOKALUPSIS: "An uncovering, manifestation. When used of a person it always denotes the appearance of the person." At Romans 8:19 the *New World* translation renders this word *revealing*.

If Jesus Christ is a person, then He must appear visibly at His coming or revelation, according to the above-quoted lexicon. *The Watchtower Society* does not attempt to answer this fact.

Another word used in this subject is EPIPHANIA. The Watchtower Bible renders this "manifestation" throughout. Regarding this word Thayer's lexicon says: "In the N. T. the 'advent' of Christ,—not only that which has already taken place and by which His presence and power appear in the saving light He has shed upon mankind, II Tim. 1:10, but also that illustrious return from heaven to earth hereafter to occur."

What will *The Watchtower* do to explain away the following text? "For the Lord himself shall descend from heaven, with a shout, with the voice of the archangel, and with the trump of God: and the dead in Christ shall rise first; then we that are alive, that are left, shall together with them be caught up in the clouds, to meet the Lord in the air: and so shall we ever be with the Lord. Wherefore comfort one another with these words" (I Thessalonians 1:16-18). Jehovah's Witnesses cannot comfort one another with these words, for they do not believe they will ever meet the Lord at all—in the air or anywhere else!

The fact that the above did not take place in 1914 as the Watchtower predicted does not prevent the Witnesses from believing the strange Watchtower interpretation on the second Coming. Read what they say in the book, *Make Sure Of All Things,* page 319: "This second presence (PAROUSIA) of Christ the Messiah was to be invisible and the unmistakable sign he gave shows conclusively that this return of Christ began in the year 1914. Since that time Christ has turned his attention towards earth's affairs and is dividing the peoples and educating the true Christians in preparation for their survival during the great storm of Armageddon, when all unfaithful mankind (all those not Jehovah's Witnesses) will be destroyed from the face of the earth."

Notice what they are saying: Jesus came down, suffered, bled and died; went back to Heaven and promptly forgot all about the whole thing, as if He lost interest! Then, suddenly, in 1914, He remembered! He recalled that there *is* a planet earth, and He began to give attention to it! *That's* how He returns, according to Jehovah's Witnesses!

In the same book certain Bible texts are used. The subject is *Return of Christ.* On page 320 they offer John 20:14-16 with the following commentary: "Appearances of Jesus After His Resurrection Made in Different Materialized Bodies." Because Mary did not recognize Jesus, they believe He took on a different body and went about incognito.

Matthew Henry's *Commentary* says regarding this incident (Volume V, page 1213). "She *knew not that it was Jesus;* not that he appeared in any other likeness, but either it was a careless transient look she cast upon him, and, her eyes being full of care (tears), she could not so well distinguish, or *they were holden, that she should not know him,* as those of the two disciples, Luke 24:16."

The book, *Make Sure Of All Things* now offers Matthew 24:3 with this comment: "Disciples Asked for Evidence of

Christ's Second Presence." In other words, their argument is: If He were to be visibly present, why the need of signs? The fact that this verse indicates that these were to be signs *preceding* His second coming eludes them when they read it.

Matthew chapter 24 clearly answers this problem. Verse 23 reads: "Then if any man shall say unto you, Lo, here is the Christ [as the Watchtower Society does right now], or there; BELIEVE IT NOT." We are plainly told that, if in the midst of the events foretold in Matthew 24 someone says that Christ is present (as Jehovah's Witnesses are saying) WE ARE NOT TO BELIEVE IT!

We are told that the second Coming will be in this manner: "For as the lightning cometh forth from the east, and is seen even unto the west; so shall be the coming of the Son of Man" (Matthew 24:27).

Now *Make Sure Of All Things* page 321 lists Matthew 23:39 with this accompanying comment: "Christ's Return Invisible, as He Testified that Man Would Not See Him Again in Human Form." The simple logic of the text does not get through to them. We quote their *New World* translation of the text as it is found in the book: "For I say unto you, You will by no means see me from henceforth until you say, 'Blessed is he that comes in Jehovah's name!' " In other words, they would not see Him again until His second coming, when He comes in Jehovah's name! The indication is that *then* they *will* see Him again! He said they would not see Him again *until* that time!

On page 323 *Make Sure Of All Things* quotes Matthew 24:16 under the comment: "Righteous flee to God's Mountainlike Organization." Even the most ardent Jehovah's Witness will squirm at *that* one! And even the most *gullible* Jehovah's Witness will hesitate before readily accepting it! They are referring, of course, to the Watchtower organization, the *New World Society*. The text thus commented upon reads: "Then let them that are in Judea flee unto the mountains." It used to be that those mountains represented Jehovah and Jesus to the Witnesses, but the organization changed it to mean the *organization* itself! This is a classic example of how they wrest the divine text for their own uses.

On that same page they quote Matthew 24:40-42, commenting: "Righteous Ones Taken Along to Safety at Christ's Second Presence." The text reads: "Then shall two men be in the field; one is taken, and one is left: two women shall be grinding at the mill; one is taken, and one is left. Watch therefore: for ye KNOW NOT on what day your Lord cometh." Now try to fit in the Watchtower comment given above!

This second "presence" is supposed to last from 1914 until Armageddon. The Bible admonishes us to watch, for at the second coming one will be taken and the other left. We are to watch because we DO NOT KNOW the day nor hour of His Coming. Read the above-quoted Watchtower comments, and compare with the Scriptures. Does it all make sense? If Christ's second "presence" is such a long, drawn-out affair, *at what time* during this long period are they "taken?" Ask a Jehovah's Witness questions like these and he will quickly want to go to other texts.

One of the *signs* of Christ's second "presence" is found on page 343 of this book: "Organized Clergy of Christendom and Evil Slave Manifested in Open Disobedience." Two texts are then quoted: II Thessalonians 2:3, 4 and II Timothy 3:1-4, 5. What seems to elude them here is the fact that the greatest departure from the faith began in 1872 when Charles Taze Russell began the movement that is today the *New World Society* of Jehovah's Witnesses. It has now become a *complete* departure from the original (and hence *true*) Christian faith.

We have yet *another* Greek word for *coming*. It is ERCHOMAI. As an example of how it is used, we read Matthew 25:27: "Thou oughtest therefore to have put my money to the bankers, and at my coming (ERCHOMAI) I should have received back mine own with interest." In Luke 19:23 the *New World* translation renders this word *arrival*, but in Luke 12:45 and 18:5 they render it *coming!* In Romans 15:22 the Watchtower translation renders it as *getting to*. Then in

Matthew 16:27 it is translated *come*. The verse following translates it as *coming*. The same is true at Matthew 24:44. For other uses see Mark 13:26; Luke 19:38; Revelation 1:7.

So you see why they would like to limit the discussion of Christ's second coming to the word PAROUSIA! By limiting the discussion to that one word, they make it appear as if they have the final answer to the entire subject!

You see how the Watchtower writers easily deceive their readers. It is on-the-surface superficiality, easily exposed by going beneath the surface. *The Watchtower Society* leans heavily on the lack of education of the people who become its Witnesses. Otherwise, their own people would expose this heresy! The Society first impresses the new follower with the organization, and after that has been accomplished, he eagerly believes anything *The Watchtower Society* tells him.

The hope of the Christian in this present day is that Christ is coming soon again. He will then receive unto Himself the redeemed. Mark 13:26 from the *New World* translation reads: "And then they will see the Son of man COMING in clouds with great power and glory." John 14:2, 3 tells us: "In my Father's house are many abiding places; if it were not so, I would have told you; for I go to prepare [HETOIMAZO] a place for you. And if I go and prepare a place for you, I come again, and will receive you unto myself; that where I am, there ye may be also."

The Bible closes with this promise: "He who testifieth these things saith, Yea: I come quickly. Amen: come, Lord Jesus" (Revelation 22:20).

The Watchtower Society holds that the very men who wrote these Scriptures were deceived, because they did not understand them as the Witnesses do today! This deception continued, they tell us, until the Watchtower Society came along to straighten it all out. They hold that the Church of Jesus Christ, which He died to redeem, fell. Then, for nearly 2000 years it remained in darkness.

Their accusations against the Church are as many as their accusations against Christ's Deity! We have seen what they think of the Saviour, and what they think of the historic faith. Now it behooves us to consider at length exactly what they think of the Church as a body.

Chapter Seven

WATCHTOWER ACCUSATIONS AGAINST THE CHURCH

A BOOKLET called *Memorandum in Reference to the Classification of Jehovah's Witnesses Under the Acts and Regulations (Selective Service System)*, from which we quote extensively in chapter 9, says on page four: "Since the beginning of their modern-day organization Jehovah's Witnesses have been called various names. Their enemies and uninformed persons have falsely called them a 'sect', naming them Russellites . . . ."

Quoting now from *Golden Age* magazine of March 17, 1920, page 409, headline: "RUSSELLISM WILL NOT DOWN. For Many Years It has Thrived on Persecution and Is No Stranger Before the Courts of the Land. Russellites—What and Who They Are." Then an editor's note reads: "This article, including an interview with Judge Rutherford, PRESIDENT OF THE RUSSELLITE ORGANIZATIONS, was at our solicitation kindly contributed . . . ."

So, according to the Selective Service booklet, "Judge" Rutherford was an "uninformed enemy" of Jehovah's Witnesses! Otherwise he would never have permitted them (and himself) to be known as "Russellites!" But Jehovah's Witnesses *are* Russellites whether they like it or not. They still parrott the old Russellite heresy.

The Watchtower Society frequently quotes men of their own religious kind (unsaved) as representative voices of the Christian church. For instance, *The Watchtower* magazine of February 15, 1954 quotes "the pastor of New York's Riverside Church, Robert J. McCracken, as reported in the New York *Times* of July 13, 1953 . . . ." However, we must note

101

that this man can only speak for the LIBERAL portion of the Church.

Now in the February 1st issue, page 79, we read:

> "Of course I do not believe in the Virgin Birth, or in that old fashioned substitutionary doctrine of the Atonement; and I do not know any intelligent Christian minister who does. The trouble with these fundamentalists is that they suppose that unless one agrees with them in their doctrinal set-up, he cannot believe in the profound, substantial, everlasting truths of the Christian gospel that transform men's lives. . . ." *Christian Beacon,* May 9, 1946, Vol. XI, No. 13 (Harry Emerson Fosdick).

The above-quoted men are *liberals.* The Protestant Church is divided mainly into these two camps—Liberal and Conservative. The "fundamentalists" mentioned in the article above are included in the Conservative category, but Jehovah's Witnesses are *not.* Notice how they quote Dr. Fosdick as if he were speaking against *them.* The Witnesses do not believe in substitutionary Atonement any more than Dr. Fosdick does! But the "fundamentalists" *do!* The Witnesses are as far from being fundamentalists as it is possible to get. If you should doubt this, it is suggested that you contact the Independent Fundamentalist Churches of America office in Chicago. No one who denies the Deity of Jesus Christ can be classified as fundamental, conservative or evangelical.

Neither the Liberals nor Jehovah's Witnesses are saved. The conservatives preach the redemptive gospel, the liberals preach a non-redemptive religion. The Watchtower "gospel" is non-redemptive. The difference between the Watchtower organization and the liberal churches is that the churches have freedom of thought and speech, whereas the Witnesses do not. It must be noted that the liberals do *not* speak for the conservatives (or evangelicals), whose message is radically different from theirs.

It is therefore most unfair for *The Watchtower* magazine to quote liberals as representative spokesmen for the entire

Protestant Church. Even more unfair is it for *The Watchtower Society* to classify themselves as Fundamentalists! They are in no wise conservative in their theology. The Witnesses make an *appearance* as if they do believe in the fundamental foundation-truths of the Gospel. Any who fall for this are making a big mistake. Search out their doctrine, and you will find it to be non-redemptive.

As mentioned in the last chapter, Jehovah's Witnesses believe that Christianity fell after the apostles were gone and did not recover until Pastor Russell came along. In *Awake!* magazine of February 8, 1960, we read from page four:

> This (apostasy) should not surprise us, as both Jesus and his apostles foretold it. The facts of history, particularly from the time of Constantine on and up to modern times, leave no doubt that such an apostasy took place. . . . Recovery from apostasy waited until the latter part of the nineteenth century. It was at that time that a group of sincere and dedicated Christians (Russellites) gathered themselves for the study of God's Word, at the same time divesting themselves of the creedal and sectarian chains of Christendom.

What do the Witnesses think of the Jews? Well, they think that *they* themselves are the *real* Jews! Why so ? They *spiritualize* all texts applying to Israel, and call themselves the "spiritual Israelites." They argue that the word *Jew* means "worshipper of God." Naturally, they believe that *they* are the only worshippers of God! Therefore, they believe that they are Jews! They spiritualize all the promises made to Israel and apply them to themselves.

We can see exactly where Jehovah's Witnesses fit into the religious scene. It is not a position to be envied! In the course of the past six chapters we have seen basically what the original, historic Christian faith is. We have defended the abiding "faith of our fathers," i.e., the faith of the Church in contrast to the faith of individual persons. But *The Watchtower* changes to suit the times, to please their readers.

Let us quote *The Watchtower* magazine of May 15, 1950:

The clergy of Christendom and millions of their religious followers claim to be Christians. They are not living up to the name. By claiming to be Christians, they assume the obligation to witness to Jehovah's name through Christ Jesus. They take the name Christian, but do they measure up to it? No! They decline to be witnesses of Jehovah.

This same issue further states:

The clergy of the various sects and cults of organized religion in Christendom call themselves by high-sounding titles. They assume these grandiose titles so as to distinguish themselves from and place themselves above the common people. . . . The clergy of Christendom have falsely assumed the name Christian. Therefore they are guilty of impersonating the first witness of Jehovah, the Lord Christ Jesus, in violation of the law of Almighty God.

Here they say that a person taking the name Christian is impersonating Christ Jesus! Jehovah's Witnesses think they are being like Jesus when they teach their heresy.
Further we read:

The clergy of Christendom and their supporters deny the second presence of Christ (see chapter six). . . . Furthermore, they teach the people that when man dies he goes to an eternal torment of hell if wicked. . . . The clergy, moreover, fail to live up to the name unlawfully assumed by them by falsely telling the people that man has a soul distinct and separate from the body. . . . Roman Catholic clergy instruct the people that man goes to "purgatory" upon death and remains in that transitory state until, by the payment of an adequate sum of money made to the priests by the relatives or friends, he is prayed out of "purgatory" into heaven.

They go on to state:

The clergy and their followers have rebelliously declined to be disciplined. . . . The actions and doctrines of the clergy of Christendom find no support in the Bible. . . . They have lied and uttered false words concerning the purposes of God.

In *Golden Age* magazine of May 20, 1925, page 524, an item appeared entitled "Scriptural Names for Apostate Clergymen." Here are some of the names contained in the list that follows: *Overthrowers of Kings; Unauthorized Ambassadors of God; Wolves in Sheep's Clothing; Vomit-Eating Dogs; Den of Serpents; Men Full of Ravening and Wickedness; Fruitless Fig Trees; Vineyards of Sour Grapes; Seed of the Devil's Sowing; Trees twice Dead; Fools; Extortioners; False Proclaimers of Peace; Justifiers of Themselves Before Men; Blind Guides; Children of the Devil,* etc.

Let us look at a typical Watchtower contradiction. In the booklet on the Selective Service System (*Memorandum*) quoted previously, we note the following on page 13:

> A prominent factor of the Reformation was a violent reaction against the dogmas and abuses of the Roman Catholic system of ordination. Without exception Protestants rejected the "five sacraments" of the Roman Catholic Church as fictitious. Almost all such churches forsook those ordination ceremonies during the Reformation and fell back on the Scriptural precedent as their sole guide for modes of appointing and ordaining ministers.

But that is not the story the book *What Has Religion Done For Mankind?* tells. On page 296 this book states: "This was no true reformation. This was not a return to the primitive Christianity of the apostles and the early Christian congregation." You see the Government is supposed to believe *one* thing, and the common people *another!*

The Watchtower also leads the people to think that no one ever heard about "Jehovah" except from Jehovah's Witnesses. The Witnesses are told that it is their assignment to tell everyone about it. They think their Society is the fountainhead of truth, and outside of their fold there is nothing but darkness.

In their meetings they repeat these things one to another, and thus continually "brainwash" each other into the "party line" of the moment.

Most people are disgusted with the Witnesses and refuse to talk to them when they come to their doors. Thus, their arguments go unchallenged many times. This encourages them and leads them to believe that there is no answer to their message. They conclude therefore that they speak the truth. They feel encouraged and strengthened in their misled faith.

We now answer them on the name "Jehovah," and from a quite unexpected source. They think knowledge of the name "Jehovah" makes them special people. This was not even God's name at all. It is from the Latin translation of the tetragrammaton YHWH. The Witnesses think it great enlightment to have come upon that name.

In the foreword to their *New World Translation of the Christian Greek Scriptures,* page 25, they state: "While inclining to view the pronunciation 'YAHWEH' as the MORE CORRECT WAY, we have retained the form 'Jehovah' because of the people's familiarity with it since the 14th century." (Emphasis mine.)

With that in mind, we quote from *A Catholic Commentary on Holy Scripture* (1953), on Exodus 3:14, 15:

THE DIVINE NAME YAHWEH. The name has two forms: *Ehyeh* "I am" used by God or an envoy speaking in his name, and *Yahweh* "He is" used by his worshippers. . . . The name therefore expresses essential existence or aseity, the radical attribute of God by which he is most adequately distinguished from created beings. . . . In the post-exilic period Adonai "Lord," or less frequently Elohim "God," was substituted through reverence for Yahweh, which was retained in the text but not read. Hence the LXX *Kurios,* the Vg "Dominus" and the hybrid form Jehovah, an erroneous combination of the consonants of one word and the vowels of another.

Further, we quote from page 549, which brings to mind the discussion of Messiah as "mighty God":

> Names in the Bible often express nature or attributes; *cf.* of the divine name, Yahweh, Ex. 3:14. . . . The sense is practically the same whether we render "a counsellor of wonderful things" or "a wonder of a counsellor." Mighty God appears always in the OT and even in Isa. 10:21 as a name of Yahweh expressing his omnipotence. The divine attribute predicated of the Messiah implies his divinity.

As to when this name was first revealed, page 165 states:

> There is still discussion whether God then revealed his sacred name Yahweh for the first time (at the Burning Bush), Ex. 3:15. The text strongly suggests that Moses knew or suspected that God was known among his countrymen by a name that was unknown to him. He had lived all his life away from them, at the court of Pharaoh's daughter and in Madian. He seems to have foreseen the incredulity if he could not tell his people the name of God who had sent him.

Jehovah's Witnesses are familiar with the expression "Jehovah God" (or *Yahweh God*) and believe that they are the only persons under the sun familiar with it! Keeping in mind that the Watchtower Society recognizes the superiority of YAHWEH over the Latin JEHOVAH, we quote again the *Catholic Commentary on Holy Scripture,* now on page 170:

> Sometimes we find Yahweh, the personal name by which God was known to the Israelites, and sometimes Elohim, the general name for God, used also of false gods. . . . The combination of the two names, Yahweh Elohim, is found exclusively in Gen. 2 and 3 except for Ex. 9:30, where the equivalent of Elohim is not in LXX and is probably not original in HT. . . . If it is true that the name Yahweh was previously unknown, then it follows that its earlier occurrences in the text of the Pent. were not original in the stories of Gen. as handed

down to the time of Moses. And this would be true also of the proper names, such as Jochabed, that of Moses' mother, in which the Tetragrammaton forms an element. . . .

It is impossible to explain the choice of one name rather than the other in all cases, just as it is impossible always to assign a reason why we sometimes speak of Jesus, sometimes of Christ, sometimes of Jesus Christ, sometimes of our Lord. To some extent the matter is fixed by usage, as we speak of "the blood royal" but never "the throne royal." So the Hebrews spoke of "a man of God" (Elohim), not of "a man of Yahweh." On the other hand "Blessed be Yahweh" is the regular expression (25 times), "Blessed be Elohim" occurring twice only, Ps. 65 (66) 20 and Ps. 67 (68) 26 both in the Elohistic section of the Psalter. . . . With the non-Israelites the name Yahweh is as a rule avoided.

As to why the name was eventually dropped from usage, the *Commentary* states page 736:

The proper name of the God of the Hebrews as Yahweh. . . . It is uncertain when its use was abandoned; it seems to have occurred between the 5th and 3rd cent. B.C. Nor is it easy to assign a reason for this avoidance of the traditional name. The opinion that it was due to an exaggerated fear or reverence is not accepted by many modern scholars. Some believe it was to protect the name from profanation by use in magical formulae; others, that it was abandoned from a monotheistic scruple.

The deities of heathendom were distinguished from one another by their personal names (Zeus, Apollo, Aphrodite, etc.); in order that the God of the Hebrews might not be esteemed one of the many, his distinctive personal name was suppressed by the more universal "God" or "Lord." Yet even these designations were used with restrictions. "God" (elohim) is not used outside the Bible. "Lord" (*adonai*, Gk *kyrios*) is used only in the Bible and in prayer.

As to Jesus Christ and His superiority over the angels, particularly as found in Hebrews 1, the *Commentary* says, page 1160:

> It is to the elevation of Christ "in the glory which was his before the world was" that his superiority above the Angel ministers of Mosaic revelation is attached. Hence the participle *genemenos: "having been made."* The distance of his superiority is seen in "the *better* name" which he "has inherited," for he is now established in possession of the glory of his Sonship, *cf.* Phil. 2:11, where "the name" is not *Son* but *Kyrios,* that is, Yahweh—with no real difference of sense, however.

Yet more on this: We note the following found on page 1027:

> The Messias is the cornerstone of the New House of Israel. Salvation comes through the Person of our Lord, all mention of the law being conspicuously absent, and it is perhaps implied that the saving name of Yahweh has been superceded by the Holy Name.

Commenting specifically on Philippians 2:10, 11, page 1129 states:

> There is a reference to Is. 45:23: "to me every knee shall bow, every tongue shall swear," where we should say in English, "by me every tongue shall swear." Absolute Godhead is asserted in Isaias and is here ascribed to Christ. But for "swear" Paul substitutes "confess," and goes on to give what is to be the subject of that confession. As Christ has suffered in his sacred humanity, so he is to be glorified for ever in that humanity, which is to receive divine adoration in virtue of the Divine Person who has assumed it.
>
> Every tongue is to "confess that Jesus is Lord, to the glory of God the Father." Possibly we should translate with Vg "in the glory," for it seems to make rather better sense of the special allusion to God the Father, and there is no doubt that the preposition *eis* with the accusative (as in the Greek here) could at this period bear this sense. . . .

Every tongue is to confess that "Jesus Christ is Lord," which is the confession of Christ's Godhead, since the Jews did not use the proper name of God, Yahweh, but spoke and read "the Lord" in its place, a practice followed by Vg and all except some modern versions.

On page 564 the *Commentary* observes:

YAHWEH ALONE IS GOD, IDOLS ARE VAIN. Idolaters have no profit from their idols. Their witnesses, as contrasted with Yahweh's, are confounded, seeing no exploit, knowing no prediction of their gods.

The Watchtower Society is critical of the Catholic Church for claiming infallible interpretation of the Bible. *The Watchtower* states that no Catholic may accept a Biblical text apart from the interpretation the Church puts upon it. According to the *Commentary* quoted above, the Catholic Church claims infallible interpretation of only some twenty texts of Scripture.

Compare this with *The Watchtower Society's* hold on the Bible of *complete* interpretation, from Genesis to Revelation! The reason for their "right" of infallible interpretation is obvious: If a Jehovah's Witness accepts some other interpretation aside from the Watchtower, it could upset the entire Watchtower organization.

The Witness is led to think he is in "God's organization" and that his overlords alone possess the right of Bible interpretation. The Witness may *read* the Bible, but only through the interpretation of the Watchtower publications! To him the Bible is a closed book apart from the Watchtower Society's printed material!

As for the Watchtower's claim that Protestant denominations are unfamiliar with the divine name of Jehovah: If the Witnesses would tune in Protestant broadcasts, or go to church, they would find out how well-known the name is. But the Witnesses have blinded themselves to the facts. They have withdrawn from Protestant churches which they now only criticize and condemn. As Watchtower addicts, they are certainly not Christians! They are prey of a Society that has deceived them, and they are apparently content to be deceived. Being blind they are willfuly led by others as blind as they themselves are.

Note that *The Watchtower* organization did not get the name JEHOVAH'S WITNESSES until 1931. Up until then the thousands who were part of the organization lived and died without knowing they were supposed to be Jehovah's Witnesses!

Later, in 1935, strict control called "theocratic organization" was exercised over every congregation throughout the world. The Society became authoritarian and the Witnesses became Watchtower slaves. They were kept within the organization by means of false promises which never materialized! It is the same today.

Above all else it is the misconception that *The Watchtower Society* is the "servant" of Matthew 24:45, 46 that keeps the Witnesses in fear of the organization. Once this fear is broken, the Witness may begin to think and to pray for himself as an individual to his heavenly (not organizational) Father.

Jehovah's Witnesses make much of the fact that Paul the apostle taught from house to house in Ephesus (Acts 20:20), ignoring the fact that the apostles used other methods as well. They conclude therefrom (wrongly) that *all* Christians *must* go from house to house or be condemned. They believe that no one is a Christian unless he goes with the message from door to door.

This type of activity is necessary for *them,* as it is the main thing that keeps their organization going. Without it, the whole thing would stop. In the absence of the Holy Spirit they substitute *organizational* spirit. They cannot possibly be guided as individuals by the Holy Spirit, for in order to be Witnesses they must reject His ministry. Thus they are regimented, for regimentation is necessary in lieu of the guiding hand of the heavenly Father. The Witnesses *must* be kept on the organizational treadmill, and may not be allowed to stop and think for themselves. Otherwise they might begin to reason: "What is the purpose of all this door-to-door drudgery?" Then they could lose interest in their worthless cause, and the Watchtower treadmill would come to a stop!

The true Church does not depend as heavily upon door to door work as Jehovah's Witnesses do, because God is director of the true Church. The true Church does not depend upon its own ability to argue in order to get converts. According to Watchtower reasoning, a prospect will be eternally lost (out of existence, to them) if some Witness does not have the ability to argue him into the Watchtower organization! Therefore their entire program depends totally on the Witness!

Would God call men to *freedom* through these slaves? The Jehovah's Witnesses are not allowed to accept the Bible as it reads, not allowed to go to church, not allowed to enter the Armed Forces, not allowed to take or give blood transfusions, not allowed to salute the flag, not allowed to worship the Saviour Jesus, not allowed to become born again—and they think they are *free!* To them it is as if the Bible reads, "The truth shall bind you hand and foot!"

They accuse Christians generally of being hypocrites. They say Christians go to church on Sunday and then live sinfully during the week. Well, I have never known a Jehovah's Witness to live otherwise! Their accusation is age-old and does not prove a thing. If we point out the hypocrisy of Witnesses, they will say that they are not *real* Witnesses, that's all! If a Christian is not living as a Christian should, then we could say he is not a *real* Christian, that's all! What does the whole argument prove? Nothing.

But there is a difference between the two. The Christian may lose some of his reward because of his failures, but his sins are covered by the blood of Jesus Christ. He will plead no works of his own to merit his own self-justification, but will plead the work of Christ for him as a sinner saved by grace. He comes not before a judgment of condemnation

(KRISIS) , but before a judgment (BEMA) of rewards for the justified.

Where will the Jehovah's Witness stand? He never received the blood of Jesus Christ as an atonement for his sins. He comes as an unsaved sinner pleading works done in the organization as price for his salvation. He expects these works to pile up a "treasure" that will at least count as part payment toward his salvation. (The other part he believes was paid by Jesus.) Not only is the Jehovah's Witness unsaved, but he thinks he will never even have to face God's judgment. He thinks he can go on and on and sin, sin, sin and then go to sleep and never answer or pay for a single sin. He brings himself to think this because he knows what final judgment is coming if he is wrong! Deep down in his heart he knows that if he has to stand before Deity someday in judgment, he will be condemned.

At that final judgment he will find that he had set himself in opposition to Christ who died for him. What an awakening *that* will be! He who scoffed at eternal punishment will find little at which to mock. Suddenly eternal fire will no longer be the subject of his scoffing, as he finds himself in it, crying out for mercy!

Jehovah's Witnesses delight in comparing the Church of Jesus Christ with everything abominable. To what kind of people do the Witnesses compare? Consider the following resemblance:

In *The Reader's Digest* of March 1960, we read of a cult posing the biggest problem to the race situation in America, headed by a man whom his followers call "The Messenger of Allah." The article carried the title, *Mr. Muhammad Speaks.* It describes this Muslim-like cult which thrives on hate; hatred of the white man and of Christianity. Their centers of learning are patterned after Islam. Note carefully what the author of the article writes as to his experiences:

> I went to Harlem's Temple of Islam No. 7, the next
> Sunday afternoon. Facing us there was a blackboard;

painted on it was an American Flag, captioned "Slavery,
Suffering, Death;" opposite it was an Islamic Star and
Crescent, captioned "Freedom Justice, Equality." Printed
between the two was, "Which One Will Survive the War
of Armageddon?"

To Jehovah's Witnesses also a nation's flag represents
slavery, suffering and death. To the Jehovah's Witness the
Watchtower organization represents freedom, justice, equality. And he believes his organization will survive the war of
Armageddon.

Jehovah's Witnesses everywhere accuse the churches and
pastors of being money-mongers. They object to the passing of the collection plate. But the Watchtower itself goes
tax free as a CHARITABLE ORGANIZATION. YET, THEY HAVE NEV-
ER GIVEN ONE CENT TO CHARITY! Why the authorities let them
get away with this is beyond comprehension.

Occasionally they pretend to be charitable. They will get
the Witnesses to contribute clothing to be sent to other Witnesses in foreign countries. *The Watchtower Society* acts as
expediter, paying shipping charges only! The Society never
has contributed a penny to charity and never will.

Jehovah's Witnesses will insist that their method of placing
literature with the public is not *selling*. All pioneers and
other full-time workers get the bound books for about 10¢
each which in turn are sold for about 50¢ each! All other
workers pay about 45¢ and sell them for about 50¢ each. Is
this not a legal *sale?*

The Witnesses plead that they give some literature away
free. Granted—they do. But that does *not* prove that their
stated "contribution" is not the "price" of the book. The
size of the "contribution" is not left to the one accepting the
literature; it is determined by the Witness himself.

When they approach a person at his door, they tell him
that he should be broadminded enough to read their literature. Yet, the Witnesses themselves will very seldom accept
literature *free* from anyone else! They refuse to read anything except their own propaganda! When Christians or

others try to get them to read Christian literature, the Witnesses reply that they have something better to read! They try to force their propaganda on others while refusing to listen to anyone or anything else. Is this as broadminded as they expect others to be?

Jehovah's Witnesses will not take blood transfusions or permit their children (infants or otherwise) to receive blood. At times they stand by idly while their children die. Thus they sacrifice their own children on the Watchtower altar of sacrifice. But they in turn refuse the sacrifice of His Son which was given for them at Calvary! They would rather do their own sacrificing than accept the sacrifice presented on their behalf.

Jehovah's Witnesses criticize churches for keeping membership rolls. Yet every congregation of Jehovah's Witnesses not only has a roll, but a complete file on each member; in the case of servants, a dossier, which is kept in New York for use if and when necessary. Each person who is a servant (equal to a board member in a church, subject only to the New York authority) comes under personal scrutiny of a traveling "circuit servant." He makes a report on the Witness, and the Witness never sees this report!

A record is kept on the pioneers on how they dress, speak, present the message, how they co-operate, how capable they are of presenting the message, what their general attitude is, how much literature they place, how many repeat visits they make, how many book studies they conduct, how many hours they spend in doing so, etc. The same goes for part-time workers except that the report is kept locally, and does not go to New York.

The Witnesses are spied upon by their own members in their conversation in the Kingdom Halls and other places where they assemble. Any suspected of being deviationists are closely watched.

Each Jehohah's Witness has seven overlords in his congregation, and seven overlords in succession within the organization, up the ladder of authority. Here are the steps up the organizational ladder: Area study conductor (area studies are known as *service centers*) ; Congregation servant; City servant; Circuit servant; District servant; Branch servant; Zone servant; Watchtower committee of seven, headed by the President. The office of City servant exists only in places where there is more than one congregation in the same town or city.

Each Witness is watched very carefully, and if anyone is suspected of deviation, he is either put on probation (limited activity and privileges) or disfellowshiped (excommunicated). If he is disfellowshiped, he is considered cast off by God! No other Jehovah's Witness in the world is supposed to talk to that person. If one does, he himself may be disfellowshiped. Some Witnesses believe that this excommunication is to be applied universally; that is, no person in the world (whether a Jehovah's Witness or not) should speak to an excommunicated Witness.

The Witnesses are led to believe that the Society cannot err when writing material for the publications. If and when the Society *later* decides such-and-such was an error, only then but not in the past can it be recognized as error. The Society decides for the Witnesses what is error. As to the argument that the Witnesses were deceived when they received such material later declared to be in error, the Society says that it was truth for the *time* (present truth), that is, it was "truth in due season," and was truth *then* but it is not truth *now!*

No Witness may ever point out an error in the Watchtower publications. They fight vehemently for what they believe. To them Watchtower doctrines are truth in spite of whatever you may show them to the contrary.

Regardless of how hard you may try to show them their error, it is usually in vain, for they are told that at the moment (as long as they are using current publications) no errors can possibly exist!

The reader may wonder just what kind of system it takes to hold people so tightly in its grip. The following chapter will give details on the various steps taken by Jehovah's Witnesses to win converts. You will follow a complete conversion, from beginning to end, and see the whole thing unfold before you. You will see how people are brainwashed before they even realize what is happening to them. Once they are convinced of this kind of thinking, only the power of Almighty God can free them from its ever-tightening chain.

Chapter Eight

THE JEKYL-AND-HYDE WATCHTOWER SYSTEM OF THOUGHT CONTROL

HOW DOES A PERSON ever get involved in such a system? How does it get a grip on him to the extent that he no longer thinks for himself? Let us begin at the beginning of the story and see what unfolds.

In most cases, persons who become Jehovah's Witnesses have had no Biblical training, or, in other cases, very little at all. Quite a number are unchurched folks seeking a faith. Their lack of Biblical knowledge pays off for the Watchtower Society which capitalizes on it. These people then become victims of one of the greatest hoaxes of our generation. How is this accomplished?

Initially, a person is called on by a Witness going from door to door. The Witness identifies himself as a *minister,* and proceeds to deliver a short sermon he learned from an instruction sheet sent him from New York headquarters. If he is successful in his delivery, he will endeavor to place whatever literature is then being offered. It usually changes from month to month, except January to April which is a subscription period for *The Watchtower* magazine.

During the course of his "sermon" he will have pointed out the need for home Bible study. He will have shown what the lack of such study has produced nationwide. He could be called an "alarmist." If the person to whom he is speaking has any complaints against churches, he is a good Jehovah Witness prospect. The Witness will build up these complaints all out of proportion. The Witness will sound like a Bible instructor, and offer books of "Bible instruction" to be read at the householder's leisure. The Witness will promise to call back within two weeks to help solve any problems or answer questions. Actually he will call back in order to work on Step No. 2.

Now if the listener has been impressed by what he heard, he may begin to read the literature. It all depends on whether or not he is seeking something spiritual. He may be impressed by the fact that someone took time to come and speak to him about religious matters. He may also be impressed because this individual was not paid to do this work. He may begin to read the literature for any one of numerous reasons.

The Witness has just accomplished Step No. 1, and the chances are that he will return just as he promised. This time he has a longer sermon (15 to 20 minutes) that he hopes to deliver. This sermon, not a product of his own mind, was likewise learned from an instruction sheet sent from headquarters. Since it is memorized, he will, no doubt, impress the householder. He will use the Bible only for the effect it has.

The Witness will sound quite orthodox, for he is trained not to discuss anything objectionable, if it can be avoided. He must find a common, meeting ground and dwell there.

This time (Step No. 2) he will inquire whether the householder has been reading the literature. At this point he will try to indoctrinate him with Watchtower propaganda. He will use several Scriptures which he has taken out of context (or, we should say, that were taken out of context *for* him by the Society). Jumping from one verse to another, he will build his false doctrines on them. The householder, if he is not well versed in the Bible, may believe it all, not knowing how the Witness is wresting the Scriptures. If the Witness can convince him, he may find himself subscribing to *The Watchtower* or *Awake!* magazines, sent twice a month (each) to fill his mind with current Watchtower heresy.

With this visit, or after several more if necessary, the Witness will pave the way for Step No. 3—the "home Bible study." He will attempt to get permission to come one day or evening and spend an hour with the householder in order to study some Watchtower-chosen topic. The householder will probably think it is to be a genuine *Bible* study. He does not realize what this will lead to, at this point. If the Witness can successfully swing this (and they have subtle ways of doing so), then Step No. 2 has been dutifully accomplished and Step No. 3 now awaits its beginning.

As promised, the Witness will show up on the night set aside for this study. The Witness knows that this is a BOOK study, but the householder thinks it is to be a BIBLE study. The topic (s) discussed will be taken from a current Watchtower publication, most likely *Let God Be True,* and the Bible will be used by the Witness as a reference book to the Watchtower publication. What appears to be a "Bible study" now begins. Step No. 3 is in full swing.

This is the crucial period in the system of brainwashing that one must undergo in order to become a Jehovah's Witness. If he goes along with this Bible-book idea (and many people pursuing such study seem to), all his former ideas and convictions will seen be washed away in a flood of Watchtower scoffing and ridicule. The book will use portions of the Scriptures and build thereupon a foundation of heresy. Yet, it appears to the casual observer that this is actually a *Bible* study!

The Witness will show the householder that God revealed Himself as *Jehovah.* He then tells his listener that no one else knows this except Jehovah's Witnesses. He will turn to Isaiah 43:10 where the name *Jehovah* and the words *servant* and *witnesses* appear. He relates this to Matthew 24:45, 46, and says the *servant* (singular) of Matthew is the *servant* in Isaiah, composed of *witnesses* (plural). On these two texts he builds the Watchtower foundation. The one being so instructed may not know what to answer. He permits the Witness to explain that this means *The Watchtower Bible and Tract Society,* whose members are called *Jehovah's Witnesses.*

The above material is essential doctrine for beginners. When he has accepted this, he is well on the way to membership. He may soon lose his identity completely in the Watchtower system of thought control. This doctrine tests his susceptibility to thought control. If it works, well and good for the Witness. Now that he has come this far, accepting *The Watchtower Society* as "the faithful and wise servant," the Jehovah's Witness will approach with Step No. 4.

He is now invited to meet with a neighborhood group of people who are likewise in the same phase of brainwashing. These groups are called the *area study centers* or the *area service centers*. They differ in size according to the locality, from three or four to fifteen or twenty members. The meetings are usually held in private homes. Here the newcomer meets other Jehovah's Witnesses as well as others who are just learning, as he is. He is told he may ask questions on difficult matters. However, when these difficult matters arise and he questions, he is told to wait until the end of the study for the answer. The Witnesses hope he will forget about it during the course of the evening's study. If he insists on an answer after the study is over, he will be given one from the Watchtower literature, not from the Bible.

Now Step No. 5, and it should come easy at this point for it is simply going to the meetings at the Kingdom Hall. This new-found person of *good-will* (that is the name tagged on such folks) is now taken to the Kingdom Hall, where he receives a welcome that varies with the locality. The members may all put on a special act in order to impress him. Then again, they may more or less ignore him. Usually an effort is put forth (even if it takes their last ounce of energy) to make him feel welcome. Then the functions of the organization will be explained to him in detail.

He is shown how the distribution of literature is handled. He is given the world-wide vision of the work to impress him even more. He will see how the Witnesses are trained in sales meetings called *service meetings,* and he will watch speakers "train" in the ministry school. If he goes on a Sunday afternoon or evening (depending again on locality), he will hear a "public lecture" which is usually dull, boring and repetitious. This will be followed by a *Watchtower study*, which is just what it claims to be—*not* a *Bible* study.

At this point Step No. 6 beckons. Once he has started attending the meetings, he will be urged to join the *theocratic ministry school*. This leads to the door-to-door work. He will be invited to go along with an experienced Witness and just listen to what is said. After that he will be invited to say a few words. Later he will take the lead while the experienced Jehovah's Witness stands by to see how well he does. Then he is on his own. The length of time this takes varies with different individuals. Some catch on quickly, others take considerable time.

Having come this far, the subject is about to reach "the point of no return"—Step No. 7. He will now be told that he must be baptized. This, the Witnesses insist, is the act of dedicating yourself to God to do His will. It will also make him an "ordained minister" with the Watchtower Society.

If he is a young man of draft eligibility age, the Society at this point will fight for him to keep him out of the Armed Forces. He will be baptized (usually with 50 or 60 others) at a *circuit assembly,* or with several hundred others at a *district assembly.* Yet he remains a sinner-unsaved, unregenerated, without his sins forgiven, with no covering by the blood of Christ. He is still in the sin he was born with, plus all those sins he has heaped upon himself during his life-span thus far. As such, he goes forth to "minister!"

A candidate can be carried through these seven steps in this manner within six months. A year can be considered the limit, with exceptions, of course. How can it all happen that fast? Consider the following reasons:

(1) A positive and favorable impression is made by the organization upon many prospective members. The Witnesses try to get all newcomers to attend one of their huge conventions, and the desired effect is usually convincing. (2) They are often impressed by the zeal and activity of the organization. (They do not appear as happy to others as they do to themselves; any outsider viewing them can see they

are a driven people.) (3) They receive knowledge, which impresses them no end. The fact that they could have gotten *better* knowledge if they had wanted it and looked for it elsewhere escapes them. (4) Many of these folks find themselves rejected socially for one reason or another, so they find "refuge" in an organization which tolerates them. The Witnesses are forced to recognize the most crude or uneducated person as their legal, social and religious equal if they come into the organization. The Society, not having to be with them as often as local Witnesses must, condescendingly tolerates them; after all, they can be of value by selling books and magazines!

The fact that the Witnesses are being made merchandise of does not disturb them. In the period of one year a person will learn all he will ever know as a Witness. If you speak to *one,* it is as though you have spoken to them *all!* Of course, you will get different answers to your questions from different Witnesses, but basically they all use the same line.

The previous chapters on doctrine have answered what the Jehovah's Witness learns basically. This little knowledge, some of which is error, is important to him. He does not know that this superficial and often false knowledge NEVER WAS, as such, the accepted doctrine of the Christian Church. He thinks these teachings were lost two thousand years ago, yet somehow originate RIGHT NOW with the Society! He believes a person would not be able to find these doctrines in the Bible alone (thus making the Bible insufficient for a person's faith), but that *The Watchtower Society* is needed to get these "new truths" in addition to the Bible.

He thinks these new-found doctrines are "truth" coming from "God's organization." From the very start he is sold the idea of ORGANIZATION. He is told that Jehovah is an ORGANIZATIONAL GOD, a "God of production" (see *The Watchtower* magazine, December 1, 1956). He is made to believe that he dare not live as an individual, but must come into *organizational relationship* with God. Thus he becomes an organization man.

The Watchtower teaches that all governments are of the Devil. *Let God Be True*, page 241 says: "The Fascist flag, the Nazi flag, and the Communist flag Jehovah's Witnesses have refused to salute. It is not that they just refuse to salute the flag of the United States and other democratic nations." Thus they put our nation's flag in the same class with the Nazi and Fascist flags. To them all government is alike, and our flag represents no more value to them than the Nazi's. They are somewhat reluctant to speak of this lest public sentiment be aroused against them over this issue. They are usually the least patriotic citizens of any community.

Yet, we note this contradiction in the booklet *Defending and Legally Establishing the Good News,* published in 1950, on page 83: "When threatened with mob violence, do not allow the officials to permit anarchy to take control of the community. Immediately call upon the state, provincial and local officials, such as the governor, mayor, sheriff and local prosecutor, to provide adequate protection." Thus they expect protection from the very governments they despise! The reason they call upon these officials is that they, not being Jehovah's Witnesses, can act in a capacity for them, namely, protection of Jehovah's Witnesses against antagonists.

Many persons have questioned this writer as to where Jehovah's Witnesses get their information against the country and the flag. Here it is—from *Let God Be True*, page 242:

> Any national flag is a symbol or image of the sovereign power of its nation. The flag of each nation is commonly regarded by it and its people who give allegiance to it as being sacred. . . . This is an act that ascribes salvation to the national emblem and to the nation for which it stands.

On page 245 we read this:

> Jehovah's Witnesses are not against people who salute or desire to salute the flag of any nation. Nor do they oppose the desire of any person to serve in the armed forces of any nation. Nor do they oppose the efforts of

any nation to raise an army by conscripting its man-
power.

Then on page 248 we read their comment made on Romans 13:1-7:

> The apostle did not intend his mention of the higher
> powers to be applied to men visible to human eyes who
> are rulers of this evil world run by Satan.

Now compare the above with this statement made in the
booklet *Defending and Legally Establishing the Good News,*
on page 88:

> We merely request that the officials treat us as the
> officials themselves desire to be treated in similar cir-
> cumstances. Practicing such policy of fairness, the offi-
> cers will not misuse THEIR GOOD OFFICES to aid and abet
> the religious fanatics and clergy who oppose the good
> news (Emphasis mine).

So, first they are the Devil's agents, then they are men holding a *good office.* Expediency again calls for Witnesses to act
friendly when they need help.

Beware, officials, every time you aid Jehovah's Witnesses,
for here is how they view such aid:

> For permitting us freedom to preach from door to
> door and publicly upon the streets the officials are prom-
> ised by Christ Jesus that they will receive this favorable
> consideration: "Verily I say unto you, Inasmuch as ye
> have done it unto one of the least of these my brethren,
> ye have done it unto me . . . And these shall go away . . .
> into life eternal." (Matt. 25:31-46) In thus granting us
> equal protection of the laws, THE OFFICIALS WILL JOIN
> US IN THE DEFENDING AND LEGALLY ESTABLISHING THE GOOD
> NEWS. (Emphasis mine.) *Defending and Legally Estab-
> lishing the Good News,* page 88.

Here they say the officials who treat them kindly will get
eternal life, although these officials do not have to become
Jehovah's Witnesses. You see how they court favor? Yet

they believe these same officials (who will get eternal life by being nice to the Witnesses) are in the *Devil's organization!* Any help is considered fighting for their cause, which is anti-government and anti-church. Needless to say, it is also anti-God and anti-Christ!

This thought-control system under which they operate is called *The New World Society.* According to the book *Faith on the March* by A. H. Macmillan (one of the top seven directors at Watchtower headquarters) 1957, Prentice-Hall, page 120, this *New World Society* began in 1919. Since then they have been propagating their tirade against all humanity, its governing processes and its religions. In this same book there appears another case of self-contradiction and duplicity. On page 173 he says, regarding the flag salute issue: "It is strictly an individual matter." Yet it is not so. The pressure of the group will prevent any Jehovah's Witness from saluting the flag. It is *not* an individual matter, but rather the organization builds up the pressure to steer him in its desired direction. His thinking, therefore, is not free but controlled, being under pressure from group-influence.

In passing, take note of page 226 of this book where we read: "Have you ever asked yourself: 'How much do I really love God? If I were to find that God's Word, the Bible, contradicted what I have always believed, which would I follow?' " Well, Jehovah's Witnesses, what have you to say? Which will it be for you now: the Watchtower or the Bible? Choose now while you are still in a situation where you may do so.

The identity of the CHARTER MEMBERS is a secret to the rank-and-file Jehovah's Witness. Few know who they are. They may be members of a local congregation without other Witnesses knowing who they are. These men act as spies when necessary, supplying information to the headquarters in addition to the usual routine procedure for such matters. More thought control! The Witness reading this may refuse to believe it, yet he may be one who himself is being spied upon! The Witness deifies the organization, and, to him, it can do no wrong.

These charter members can also be used to spread lies among the Witnesses against a particular individual if the Society so desires. All Witnesses are also permitted to perjure themselves on the witness stand in court, as long as they are protecting other Witnesses!

Anything the Watchtower Society sanctions is adopted by the Witnesses. Any doctrine passed by *The Watchtower Society* is then taught by Jehovah's Witnesses. Whatever *The Watchtower Society* says is law. The Bible is not consulted in these matters because they do not believe it is necessary! Their organization could get along without the Bible for which their own publications are substituted. To see the influence of these books upon any Jehovah's Witness, try to hold a discussion with one using only the Bible. This will ordinarily throw him into utter confusion. Thus you will see how dependent he is on Watchtower books in order to speak. On the other hand—if the Society orders him *not* to speak, he will not speak. In some cases *The Watchtower Society* has done this.

If you persuade the Witness to put away his books and converse with you using only the Bible, he will be hopelessly confused. There is probably no Jehovah's Witness who can work with the Bible alone. If you point out Scriptures he has never seen before (and there are plenty such), and if he cannot recall what *The Watchtower Society* has told him regarding them, he will have to consult his superiors before giving you an answer. His superiors now have his tongue, the tongue of one who claims to be free.

Under no circumstances is the Bible allowed to contradict Watchtower teaching. That is why they had to re-write the entire Bible. It just would not fit as it was. However, one can go only so far afield in tampering with the divine text, as has been shown in this book. Even the *New World* translation cannot hide some of the great truths that stand against their self-invented heresy. Both their Bible and their theology is decidedly for the uninformed.

Whenever they come to a difficult question on some Bible text, the Witnesses, in discussing it among themselves, will ask, "What does *The Watchtower* say?" If no answer can be found in existing publications or from other Witnesses, the usual procedure is to write to the New York headquarters for an answer to the problem. If the New York office feels like answering it, they do. Otherwise the questioner is left with the problem. If the Society fails to explain it, they will throw out the text until the time comes when *The Watchtower* decides to explain it to them.

The writer spent ten years within this system, and the facts presented are not being stretched in the slightest. As a matter of fact, some things are being withheld, as the Witnesses would never believe them anyway. They think their organization has a shot of some divine "truth serum," and is immune from telling lies, either accidently or deliberately. Their consciences are soothed by the lullaby-music of *The Watchtower Society* which constantly tells them all is well. Once sold on this Society, he is in its grip, tight as a vise.

No Jehovah's Witness is *what* he is entirely by his own choice. He thinks he is, but he is blind to facts. First, the Bible and the Watchtower literature are used together to lure him toward the organization. With all this comes the assuring words of his instructor that it is all the truth. Then, he comes under continual influence of the magazines (one each week), along with constant urging of the other Witnesses, pushing him on. He is pressured all the way, and falls under this *pressure* of the movement.

The repetitious fact suggested to him (though not in these words) is: Everybody else does it—*you* must, too! He is constantly threatened with annihilation at Armageddon if he does not conform. Strict conformity is necessary and is obvious throughout the entire organization. Thus he is pressured through conformity into becoming a Watchtower automaton. He then goes out to do unto others as he himself has been done unto.

Convincing themselves by constant repetition of their teachings, the Witnesses constantly talk themselves deeper into their beliefs. Individual thought is discouraged in order to give full authority to *Organizational Mindedness*. That is why it is so difficult for followers to break away from the organization.

The organization has become a part of their lives and their lives revolve around the organization. Deep down underneath it all is a fear of displeasing the organization. They fear the organization will shame them before other Witnesses if they do not obey.

Here are more proofs of what makes the Witnesses the way they are. From the book *Qualified To Be Ministers* published in 1955, on page 86: "The meetings conducted by Jehovah's Witnesses are the most important meetings that take place on the face of the earth." What do they do at such meetings? For one thing, they demonstrate how to place *The Watchtower* magazine. Here are recommendations for doing such, as found on page 184: "Sometimes it is helpful in placing subscriptions to take along several issues. A display of the different colors is attractive." And these are the most important meetings on the face of the earth! This indeed is encouragement for people with childish minds to remain that way.

Here is one that is humorous: "Jehovah's theocratic ministers are always courteous and polite in their dealing with all persons, whether of the public or government officials and officers of the law." Any person who has ever confronted a Jehovah's Witness will easily see through *that* statement. Especially are they rude and most impolite to persons having a zealous faith different from their own, and who are using public methods for imparting their message to others. The reason is that the Witnesses covet freedom to impart their own religion without granting the same freedom to others. If they had their way about it, all others would be excluded from this freedom.

Now for the benefit of the non-Jehovah's Witness reader of this book, the following is presented to show you how Jehovah's Witnesses are trained to deal with you. In *Qualified To Be Ministers*, page 193, we read the following contained in the chapter "Approaching Persons of Varied Faiths."

> We may approach a person who does not specify that he belongs to any particular faith, but merely states, "I have my church." The best way to deal with such a person is to get him talking [but just try to get a word in while a J. W. is talking!], to show interest in his church [such interest being feigned] and what he thinks and get him to express a few things that he believes. One might ask him what the person thinks of the movement toward union of all religions, then show the danger here in compromising beliefs [none of which are true, according to the J. W. anyway!] and principles for the sake of mere unity.

There is real psychology behind all this. He appears to agree with you, while in reality he disagrees with you. Here are further instructions:

> Again we may have a territory in which there are many Catholic people. We can express our [feigned] pleasure in meeting Catholics [another clever deception used on unsuspecting Catholics], and make a statement such as this, "I know Catholics are great believers in Christ." Or say, "I have many good discussions with Catholics."

Whether he does or not, he is supposed to say this. You see how he is NOT SPEAKING HIS OWN THOUGHTS, but the thinking that the Watchtower has put into his head. All of his statements can be traced to existing Watchtower publications.

Regarding their approach to Jews, this book suggests:

In speaking with these it is better to use mainly the Hebrew Scriptures, talking about Abraham and the covenant made to him, then describing the wonderful Kingdom promises outlined by the prophet Isaiah and the rising up of Messiah, as mentioned in Daniel.

Further along, the same chapter states:

Many times they the [Jews] can be appealed to to accept the Watchtower publications because of their educational content and because much of the history of the Jewish nation, also the chronology and things relating to their ancestors, are dealt with in the literature.

Needless to say, the Jewish people can find better and more accurate reading material on such matters among their own publications than they will ever get from *The Watchtower Society.*

Page 199 of this book suggests:

Get as many agreements as possible from your opponent. That way your opponent will not be aware that you are out to convert him.

The instructions continue:

Shun involved, technical arguments. For instance, if you are disproving the trinity doctrine, use proofs such as John 14:28; 5:19; 20:17, and illustrations of Jesus praying to Jehovah as his God, instances of proof where Jesus is shown as subject to Jehovah God, such as I Corinthians 15:27, etc. These would convince the average honest person who would reason [not *believe*], and usually the good-will person will be convinced by such lucid arguments. On the other hand, weak arguments on side issues give your opponent a chance to shift ground or get off onto a minor, insignificant technicality.

This procedure works well on some who do not know the Bible well. Notice how it assures the Jehovah's Witness that anything deviating from this prescribed course is a *technicality*, or a "side issue." The Witness is thus led to believe that only HIS arguments are solid, and all others are weak and insignificant. In other words, it is a foregone conclusion with him that he is always right and others are always wrong, regardless of what the topic may be.

In the above-quoted book *The Watchtower Society* compares Jehovah's Witnesses with the early Christians—a most unfair, ridiculous comparison. On page 283 they quote Charles Samuel Braden, in *These Also Believe,* published in 1950: " 'To argue successfully with them on Scriptural grounds, one must know his Scriptures better than most members of even the fundamentalist churches do today.' " This, then, is the challenge! It is also the answer—right from their own mouth.

At the end of an article setting forth their own version of the history of the Church, we read on page 295 of the above-quoted book:

> Comes the nineteenth century, and numerous religious sects and diversions rise throughout "Christendom." The major Protestant systems had by now become thoroughly organized and set, resisting any further changes and development. They, too, set about to hinder further enlightenment and growth of the truth of the Holy Scriptures.

The reader should by now be able to discern what the Witness' attitude toward him is when he is confronted at his door. You now know what is behind that casual smile and attitude he wears. You now see the training he has received and you know already what he thinks of you. Now you realize exactly what he wants.

On page 360 this book states: "They [Jehovah's Witnesses] know the New World Society will go through Armageddon fully organized and will expand until it fully covers the entire earth." This means, of course, the obliteration of all but themselves. There will be no faith but theirs and no room for any other persons except themselves.

Despite the flowery language quoted so far, the Witnesses

stand against all government and all churches remains unchanged. *The Kingdom Is At Hand* says on page 367: "Unwisely refusing instruction from Jehovah's Word, the self-seeking governing powers of earth are toying with destruction for themselves by Jehovah's King at the battle of Armageddon." Remember what the Witness is supposed to say when he confronts you? There you see the two-faced system under which he operates. He must APPEAR to agree with you although he really does not.

The Watchtower-published book *What Has Religion Done For Mankind?* (1951) page 319, informs the Witnesses:

> Christendom's religion in all its sectarian forms is an apostasy, a falling away from the pure, primitive Christianity based on God's holy Word the Bible. It has rejected God's kingdom set up at the enthronement of the Seed of his woman, Jesus Christ. As an organized, collective system of religion its clergy are the "embodiment of disobedience" to Jehovah God.

Summing it all up, the conclusion appears on page 322, stating:

> Communists with their Red religion and the clergy of Christendom—which class is the more reprehensible? The Bible answers, The religious clergy.

One further example of typical Watchtower duplicity. This writer, when a Jehovah's Witness, received a letter from Radio Moscow dated September 14, 1954, signed by I. Petrov, Radio Moscow Letters Dept. It reads:

> We have your letter of August 20th regarding freedom of worship for Jehovah's Witnesses in the U.S.S.R. We wish to inform you that contrary to what you have heard Jehovah's Witnesses are permitted to worship in the Soviet Union.

Pressing for further proof of this, the writer again wrote Radio Moscow and in reply received this second letter, dated October 30, 1954, which reads in part:

We have your letter of September 23rd and wish to inform you that we can add nothing to the information we already gave you about freedom of religion in the Soviet Union in our previous letter. The information that you have is biased and untrue and has nothing in common with the real state of affairs in the Soviet Union.

"The information you have" refers to this writer's assertion that Jehovah's Witnesses were not allowed to meet or perform their work in Russia, according to what *The Watchtower Society* said on the matter. Sending a photo copy of the first letter to New York with the suggestion that the Russian Government might be petitioned (getting them to back up the statements made in the letter with deeds), *The Watchtower Society* replied in a letter dated October 22, 1954:

> This is in answer to your letter of September 23 about holding the Russian Government to back up its statements that Jehovah's Witnesses are permitted to worship in the Soviet Union. . . . However, it is not apparent why any servant of Jehovah should so much as think there is a chance of the Russian Government heeding an appeal to justice. Its black record of acts against the New World Society and refusal to grant Christian pleas of Jehovah's faithful witnesses in Soviet Russia itself should convince one that no letters or representations on our part would do any good.

The Watchtower magazine of April 15, 1957, however, contains THE PETITION SENT TO THE RUSSIAN GOVERNMENT BY THE WATCHTOWER SOCIETY. Yes, therein is the petition that the Watchtower Society said would be UNTHINKABLE to any servant of Jehovah! This petition was read at 199 district assemblies of Jehovah's Witnesses. This writer heard it read in Reading, Pennsylvania. Part of this petition reads:

> DISCUSSION PROPOSED. We shall be very pleased to have representatives of our governing body, Watchtower and Tract Society, discuss this matter with you, either with

your foremost representatives in the United States of America or directly with your Government in Moscow.

So in this petition they proposed to thousands of Jehovah's Witnesses all over the world what no "servant of Jehovah should so much as think" of doing. That is typical of the Jekyl-and-Hyde method the Watchtower uses in its ministry of confusion. No wonder they lose thousands of members.

The Watchtower discourages, yes, actually destroys ambition. It brings to nought the worthiness of the individual. For the young people they discourage college and university training. For the older folks they discourage any specialized training, because they are supposed to remain slaves for the New World Society. That is why many of Jehovah's Witnesses are worthless; they know only their Watchtower-taught doctrine. They do nothing for the good of others outside their group.

They gain much publicity from their stand against the Armed Forces. But are they really and truly ministers as they claim to be when requesting draft exemption? Is the accusation true that people get into that organization just to avoid serving in the Armed Forces? Do Jehovah's Witnesses attempt to prevent our own nation's aggressiveness? These and other problems in the next chapter. We will use the booklet already mentioned. It was issued to Jehovah's Witnesses during the 1950's. The public was never shown this material. In fact, no other Witnesses except those directly involved ever get to see this material. Only one copy was issued to each person involved.

We are about to see the difference between what they tell the Government and what is really practiced. The Government is fooled, and the citizens are deceived. The Witnesses themselves, however, are the ones most greatly hoodwinked. They are led to believe that they are something which they actually are not. If they were left to think for themselves, as God intended us to do, they would soon realize how badly they had been tricked. But their minds are carefully guarded from private thinking. Thus, they are led astray.

Chapter Nine

THE WATCHTOWER SOCIETY VERSUS THE SELECTIVE SERVICE SYSTEM

SETTING FORTH the stand Jehovah's Witnesses take against the Armed Forces, *The Watchtower* magazine of February 1, 1951 says on page 77: "They [Jehovah's Witnesses] tell officials of the government that they conscientiously object to serving in any military establishment or any civilian arrangement that substitutes for military service."

We now quote a booklet bearing the title UNITED STATES OF AMERICA SELECTIVE SERVICE SYSTEM. MEMORANDUM IN REFERENCE TO THE CLASSIFICATION OF JEHOVAH'S WITNESSES UNDER THE ACT AND REGULATIONS. (SUBMITTED TO THE PRESIDENTIAL APPEAL BOARD AND MAJOR GENERAL LEWIS B. HERSHEY, DIRECTOR OF SELECTIVE SERVICE, NOVEMBER, 1950.) This was issued only to Jehovah's Witnesses who needed counsel from the Society regarding their draft classification.

Beginning on page five of the *Memorandum,* we read:

> More than 70,000,000 people in the United States do not belong to any religious organization. Many other millions do not attend any church, although they nominally belong to one of the religious organizations. These non-churchgoers are not heathen. . . . It is just as important to have primitive ministers and evangelists going from door to door to maintain the morale of these millions as it is to preserve the morale of those who attend some orthodox religious organization's church services. . . . Accordingly, these millions would starve for want of spiritual food were it not for Jehovah's Witnesses. . . .

Take note that the above material was prepared specifically for the Selective Service System's Board of Appeal. They would probably be inclined to accept what the *Memorandum* contains as truth. *The Watchtower Society* has led them to believe wrongly that Jehovah's Witnesses are "maintaining the morale" of millions of people. This is indeed humorous. These millions probably would be happier if Jehovah's Witnesses would not bother them.

Now note this interesting reading found on page six:

> It is not necessary to know theology, philosophy, art, science and ancient classic languages to preach the gospel. One is not required to wear a distinctive garb, live in a parsonage, ride in an expensive automobile, have a costly edifice in which to preach, and command a high salary, to qualify as a minister of God.

The above is said in an effort to conceal their own regimentation of Jehovah's Witnesses. Note the remark that it is not necessary for a minister to live in a "parsonage." A parsonage is another name for a house when occupied by a minister. Pray tell, where would it be best for him to live, if not in a house?

At the bottom of page 6, this *Memorandum* explains what "qualifies" a Jehovah's Witness as a *minister*. We read: "The work done by such a minister of Jehovah's Witnesses cannot be done by a lay worker. . . . Persons not ministers, except those preparing for the ministry, are not authorized to engage in such preaching activity." Here is the *truth: The Watchtower Society* issues no "authorization" to any Jehovah's Witness to preach, regardless of *what* is his stage of learning. Further, the Society does permit unbaptized (hence *undedicated*—not yet ordained) Witnesses to go from door to door and to speak from the platform in the Kingdom Hall.

Note the expression used, "preparing for the ministry." If they are thus *preparing*, how does it come about that this preparation never ends? A person preparing for something eventually reaches the place where the preparatory stage ends and he begins what he prepared to do. But not so with Jehovah's Witnesses. Even when they are "ordained" (baptized by immersion), the "preparation" does not end. Some have been "preparing" for thirty or fourty years, or longer. Actually, there is no preparation period.

Newcomers in the organization are started off as quickly as possible—after a few week's study sometimes. What "ministry" could they possibly be preparing for? The majority of them do nothing more than sell books and give short speeches in the Kingdom Hall. The only exception is the student body of the school where prospective missionaries are sent to train. This school is called *Gilead* and is located in New York State.

It is intended to appear to the Selective Service System that these students are going through a systematic study and training, preparing themselves for a standard ministry. Nothing could be further from the truth. They feel secure organizationally, however, because none from among them will tell the truth about their status. No Jehovah's Witness would dare to breathe a word of truth about this lest the Government withdraw the military exemption privileges.

Page 7 reads: "The clergy of the orthodox religions have their church buildings and edifices. Members of their congregations come there to hear them preach. Members of the congregation are not authorized or ordained to preach." To which we reply: Neither are Jehovah's Witnesses. They have no prescribed system of learning, and their academic standards are so far below that of any other "system" as to be practically valueless. There is no such thing as a progressive study among Jehovah's Witnesses. They are taught the same things over and over again in a constant cycle of repetition.

The Watchtower Society tells the Witnesses that *they* are the only ones doing their particular type of work and cannot be compared with any others. But what they tell the Government is another thing. Quoting the *Memorandum,* page 7:

The Society of Jesus (Jesuits) is an illustration of a society of ministers. Each member is an ordained priest.

... In various other missionary societies, the Baptist
Home Missionary Society, and other missionary societies
of the orthodox religious denominations, each missionary and evangelist is a minister. ... Indeed, such missionary societies operate on THE SAME PRINCIPLE AS DO
JEHOVAH'S WITNESSES. Each of such missionary evange-
lists goes from place to place, FROM HOUSE TO HOUSE. ...
(Emphasis mine.)

Yet Jehovah's Witnesses are told that they cannot be compared with any others. But notice please: The comparison
given therein, of Jehovah's Witnesses with the Jesuits, etc.,
is a decided error. No Jehovah's Witness in his lifetime de-
votes himself to serious study and preparation as one going
into the Catholic priesthood.

Recall how the Watchtower publications say that all denominations are of the Devil? Look now at this, found on
page 8 of the *Memorandum:*

Since Jehovah's Witnesses are A RECOGNIZED RELIGIOUS
DENOMINATION, it must be admitted that they are entitled
to have some ministers. It is for Jehovah's Witnesses to
decide who their ministers are. ... IT HAS BEEN SEEN
THAT JEHOVAH'S WITNESSES PREACH IN THE SAME WAY
THAT THE ORTHODOX CLERGY PREACH. (Emphasis mine.)

The above is a ridiculous paradox. Claiming first that
all denominations are of the Devil, they then choose to
be one of them, for purposes of expediency. So it is only fair
that they like others have *some* ministers. But they are *all*
considered ministers. For legal reasons they must be ministers to minister to all the other ministers.

Do they, as ministers, choose who their ministers shall be?
Any Jehovah's Witness knows this is not so. How can they
decide who their ministers are to be when they *have* no ministers? They themselves are all ministers! Therefore they do
not decide who their ministers are to be, or do they decide
that they themselves are to be their own ministers? If they
decide who their ministers are to be (as the *Memorandum*

claims), and they themselves are the ministers, then they have chosen themselves.

On page 6 we read: "Each of Jehovah's Witnesses is a minister." How can they therefore *choose* their *ministers?* How can it be said that "it is only fair that they have some ministers"? None of these "ministers" will recognize "minister" as clergy different from laity. How could one be their "minister" then, when there is no laity? On page 8 the *Memorandum* says: "There is no laity among Jehovah's Witnesses."

Why do they thus deceive the Government? Because they believe that all earthly Governments are of the Devil, and they have no guilt of conscience about lying to "the Devil's organization." Thus, casting principles aside, anything goes, as long as it accomplishes their expedient purpose.

In any Kingdom Hall you may enter, you will probably hear it said that Jehovah's Witnesses in no way resemble the clergy. They proudly boast that there is no comparison and that *they* are far above the clergy. Compare that statement with the statement that Jehovah's Witnesses "preach in the same way that the orthodox clergy preach." Of course they do not really *mean* all they say, but it keeps members from being drafted into the Armed Forces.

They also preach in the Kingdom Halls that no other religious group preaches from door to door except Jehovah's Witnesses. Yet, in the *Memorandum* on page 8 they admit that others do. On page 9 is another questionable statement:

> If he [the Jehovah's Witness] has satisfactorily completed a course of study in the Bible and Bible helps prescribed by the governing body of Jehovah's Witnesses, and has established his qualifications, that should be sufficient and conclusive upon the executive branch and judicial branch of the Government.

What qualifications? Up until 1957 this writer, while in the organization, never experienced what they here prescribe. But it was easy to get a 4-D classification (U.S. Government armed forces draft exemption) and later become a pioneer, servant, etc!

The truth of the matter is, if a member studies for a few weeks and then decides he would like to preach from door to door, no one generally stops him. Often he is never examined as to what he believes nor how well he can explain the Watchtower doctrine. He may become baptized whenever it suits him. He is then considered "ordained." So to be "qualified," all he has to do is be willing to preach anything *The Watchtower Society* gives him to preach.

You may test this sometime for yourself. Whenever two Jehovah's Witnesses come to your house together, one will most likely be "training" the other. Start to ask questions of the one who is not saying much, if anything, and see who gives the answers. You will see that the "training" is not so much on doctrine as it is in methods of approaching and convincing the householder.

Standing before the Government *The Watchtower Society* claims representation as a recognized denomination, claiming that they carry out their work in the same manner as others do. But before the Witnesses themselves, the Society's talk changes and they no longer resemble anything in Christendom. All these people and religions that they have likened themselves to in the *Memorandum* are unlike Jehovah's Witnesses in their other writings.

Now we will consider the way they represent their methods of preaching to the Government. On page 9 we read: "Indeed the literature is offered on a contribution basis." This is not true. There is a set *price* for every book, and the "contribution" must cover that price. The Witness may give literature away if he cares to, but he must pay *The Watchtower Society* for all of it. He gets nothing free from them.

On the same page, they state regarding the Seventh-Day Adventists:

> They are not ordained as are Jehovah's Witnesses. They merely sell books. They do not conduct home

Bible studies. They do not make revisits; they do not preach before congregations; they do not conduct baptismal ceremonies; they do not participate in the burial of the dead; they do not perform other ceremonies; all of which are performed by Jehovah's Witnesses. . . .

Again, this is not true!

Most Jehovah's Witnesses do not engage in the above-described activities. Many of them make revisits, but comparatively few conduct studies. Only a few preach (lecture) before the congregation. Only those specially assigned give burial discourses, perform marriages, etc. As for "baptismal ceremonies," there is no such thing in the local congregation. These discourses are given at assemblies, not locally. There is usually no more than one selected from a congregation to give funeral discourses and/or perform marriages. So, again they misrepresent themselves before the Government of the United States.

Now on page 11, under "Training and Ordination":

He must first be a student preparing himself for the ministry before he undertakes to act as an ordained minister of Jehovah's Witnesses. . . . While Jehovah's Witnesses of today do not attend any theological seminary or religious university in preparing for their ministry, neither did Christ Jesus. . . . The main textbook is the Bible. Other books and courses of instruction, free of all erroneous traditions and false dogmas, are provided. . . . Considerable time must be spent by the student preparing for the ministry before he becomes equipped to enter the ministry.

It all sounds quite orthodox to hear them tell it in the *Memorandum.* But what they say therein and what they practice are two different things. Naturally they are against seminaries and universities! Knowledge is a dangerous thing for a Jehovah's Witness! *The Watchtower Society* must guard against any real knowledge of free thought among the Witnesses. If they begin to think for themselves, they will soon find themselves thinking contrary to the rest of the organization. If Witnesses found out about the truth as taught in some schools, they would begin to wonder about the soundness of their organization. In order to keep members under tight control, the Society can allow for no other source of "truth" other than from their own organization.

On page 13 of the *Memorandum* they appear to recognize some "fellow worshippers" whom they condemn elsewhere in their literature: "Many groups, such as the Society of Friends, Disciples of Christ, Plymouth Brethren and Jehovah's Witnesses do not recognize any human right of ordination. They recognize the ordination as coming only from Almighty God Jehovah." Here again they include themselves with these groups for expediency. Apparently, they are willing to classify themselves as part of what they call "the Devil's organization" if it will serve their purpose of avoiding serving in a nation's Armed Forces.

Take note of this comparison found on page 18: "An organization operated on a theocratic basis like Jehovah's Witnesses or on a hierarchial basis like the Roman Catholic Church must have the privilege of assigning its ministers...."

One who has been in their organization and worked with it for years can only pity those who believe what is said in this *Memorandum*. The Government officials, members of the Selective Service System, the Presidential Appeal Board, etc., are not aware of the Watchtower system and how it *really* operates. They innocently believe what they are told by *The Watchtower Society*. But if they would send an incognito observer from Secret Service to go through the steps of becoming a Jehovah's Witness he would soon realize how the government had been tricked.

They would be enlightened if the authorities would investigate the secret files of the New York headquarters or the Kingdom Halls. (Jehovah's Witnesses generally do not know that certain files are kept from them and from the Government.) The intraorganizational correspondence would unveil the real workings and methods of *The Watchtower* organization.

Note the following Catholic authority quoted by *The Watchtower Society* to bolster their case before the government. In the literature distributed to the public they criticize and ridicule Catholics. But here, in the *Memorandum,* a Catholic authority is quoted as if he were speaking for the Witnesses. Page 19 reads:

> Immunity from military service is inseparable from the right of a people to religious liberty. It is not a privilege conceded unfairly to the ministers of religion as a class. In respecting the immunity of the clergy from military service the state recognizes the right of the people at all times to practice their religion and to have available for that purpose the ministrations of their priests (Right Reverend Monsignor Michael J. Ready, General Secretary of the National Catholic Welfare Conference, Washington, D.C.) .

Here they quote an authority and it would appear that the Witnesses want to be thought of as equal to priests of the Catholic Church. Monsignor Ready was defending the right of the CLERGY to military exemption—NOT Jehovah's Witnesses. Of course, in the *Memorandum,* they are trying to make it appear as if they are equal to the clergy, or the same *as* the clergy. But if a speaker in Kingdom Hall were to draw this comparison, it would make Jehovah's Witnesses shudder. On page 22 they quote a Jesuit priest for expediency. Then, before the public, these same men are held up to ridicule as members of "the Devil's organization." Such is the hypocritical method employed by *The Watchtower Society* to advance their activities.

On page 30, under "Full-Time Ministers in the Field," we read: "The circuit servants are full-time, ordained ministers. They perform duties in behalf of the Society VERY SIMILAR TO THOSE PERFORMED BY THE BISHOP OF AN ORTHODOX CHURCH." (Emphasis mine.) From the platform of the Kingdom Ha it is repeated time and time again that Jehovah's Witness including circuit servants, are different from the clergy. This difference, they believe, is what makes them Christians.

Now observe this statement, found on page 33: "The orthodox church-sustained clergy do not spend any more time in their preaching activities yet they do not sustain themselves by secular work as do these ministers."

The truth is that the average clergyman spends much more time pursuing his duties than the average Jehovah's Witness spends in his work. Jehovah's Witnesses speak of what they know not. They have withdrawn from the churches and the clergy to criticize and to mock. But they themselves remain mostly in darkness as to real Biblical Christianity. They have willfully blinded themselves to the truth. Their scorn of the clergy is based on their failure to find the facts.

On page 34 we find a quotation that is disgusting, since it is applied by the Watchtower to the work of Jehovah's Witnesses. We read: "The first formal and greatly effective organization of lay preaching as a system, and as a recognized branch of church effort, took place under John Wesley at an early period of that great religious movement known as the revival of the 18th century." Their quoting this item is simply to strengthen their case. Think of comparing themselves with the Wesleyan movement! They are as far as can be removed from what was done by the Wesleyan movement.

Trying to appear orthodox and yet giving reasons why a "minister" of theirs has to have a secular job, we read on page 35: "The mere fact that a poor preacher of a financially weak congregation is required to perform secular work during the week to support himself in the ministry does not bar him from claiming the exemption as a minister of religion. . . ." This is supposed to excuse Jehovah's Witnesses for being full-time secular workers when they claim draft exemption rights as full-time ministers.

They like to appear as defenders of freedom in order to put on a good "front" before the Government. Yet, it is only their own freedom which they are interested in protecting. On page 44 we read: "They fight for freedom on the home front of the nations of this world. [What other nations are there?] They fight to defend and legally establish the good news [their term for the heresy they preach] before courts, officials, administrative boards and other agencies of governments." Here is a clear statement of what they are fighting for. It is *their* right to preach their own message. What it amounts to is they fight the Government on the home front, in order to evade serving in the Armed Forces.

Another contradiction is found in *Golden Age* magazine of August 25, 1926 on page 765 under "Bible Questions and Answers":

> QUESTION: If the nation wherein a Christian resides should be at war with another nation, and the enemy entered my house and attacked my mother, what should I do as a Christian? ANSWER: Do exactly the same as you would do if the same thing happened in your home in a time of peace. . . . You would try to prevent it, by persuasion, and by putting yourself in her place, and by appealing to the law; BUT YOU WOULD NOT COMMIT MURDER. (Emphasis mine.)

Now the *Memorandum,* page 43:

> Jehovah's Witnesses are justified in KILLING a person that breaks into their home if it is necessary to repel the assault. (Emphasis mine.)

Now we arrive at a crucial point in this discussion. What we are about to uncover will be denied by Jehovah's Witnesses as is expected. They do not want anyone outside of their organization to know this. It is supposed to be knowledge shared only by those within the confines of *The New World Society.* Page 47 reads:

> They do not teach others of Jehovah's Witnesses or people who are not to refuse to support the armed forces or volunteer for service. It would be wrong to do so. . . . They do not, in fact, tell each other what to do or not to do. Each Witness of Jehovah decides by himself alone what course he shall take. His decision as to whether

to render to God what is God's is dictated by his individual understanding of the law of God in the Word of Jehovah, the Bible. His decision is formed not by the written word of the Society or any person among Jehovah's Witnesses.

That is what the *Government* is told. The Society is too smart to put in writing instructions they give Witnesses on this subject. They know what would happen if government officials ever laid their hands on it. The truth is, no Jehovah's Witness is allowed to have an "individual understanding" of the Bible. It is strictly forbidden in their organization. They bring pressure on individuals in order to force them to refuse service in the nation's defense system.

If a servant (there are seven in each congregation, plus subordinates) or a pioneer *should* enter the Armed Forces, he is removed from his position, from the organization itself, and looked upon as an unbeliever. Does this give the individual personal choice in the matter?

This writer, when a Jehovah's Witness, once wrote to the Society pressing for an answer to the question: What does the Society say about individuals who enter the service, or take a civilian job in place of military service? An answer came, addressed to the congregation servant. The letter went into the Kingdom Hall private file to which the Witnesses are denied access for a very obvious reason. The letter stated that such individuals are considered "immature" (weak in the faith), and are not to be allowed to represent the Society or perform works as Jehovah's Witnesses. It is stated that such persons would, for all practical purposes, be considered outsiders. Letters like this are kept secret from the government.

If any reader should doubt what is being said here, he may ask any Jehovah's Witness what happens to one of them who decides to join the Armed Services. Group-pressure is used to steer the Witness into line and into *organizational thinking*. He is free to join the service, of course. But he will be removed from the organization if he does. He can make up his own mind on the matter which is called "freedom of choice!" But if he joins up, he will be removed from what he is led to believe is *God's organization.*

Do you see how they have deceived the Government? The writer has personally known young men who, when faced with being drafted, quickly joined the "theocratic ministry school," so they could tell the draft board that they were studying for the "ministry." One such young man was not even qualified to minister from door to door alone for lack of knowledge. Yet he claimed exemption under the ministerial status. He knew almost nothing about the Bible or the Watchtower teachings. He was in the organization because of family ties. Yet he is tolerated as a member in good standing. Such is a Watchtower "minister." Yes, "preparing for the ministry" is the line used by many young men, some of whom merely are *associated* with the Watchtower organization, in order to get a draft board exemption.

On page 47 the *Memorandum* says:

> They believe it is within the province of a nation to arm itself and resist attack or invasion. It is admitted that the Government has the authority to take all reasonable, necessary and constitutional measures to gear the nation for war and so lubricate the war machinery as to keep it working effectively.

Here they say it is all right for a nation to arm itself for the defense of its citizens, who include Jehovah's Witnesses. So they are not against a nation which defends them in the event of an attack. They sanction war machinery when it is used by the nation to defend them. The nation may "resist attack or invasion," that is, *others* in the nation *besides* Jehovah's Witnesses may do this. The nation has their permission and approval to defend them, but they, themselves, will not participate in the military defense.

In other words, the nation has the right to protect its Jehovah's Witness citizens against enemy attack. But for Witnesses to do this, would be for them unscriptural. But it is very well for others in the nation to rush to their defense.

The others are *not* Jehovah's Witnesses and therefore may be unscriptural and defend the nation, and at the same time defend Witnesses.

When the Witnesses are in trouble, they depend on the army and the police, because the army and the police not being Jehovah's Witnesses can kill in defense of the Witnesses. Jehovah's Witnesses could not kill in defense of the police, but it is well if the police kill in defense of Jehovah's Witnesses.

As has already been said, any Jehovah's Witness deciding for himself to enter the Armed Forces is immediately removed from the organization, not disfellowshiped, but just dropped from the rolls. So it *is* true—they *may* decide for themselves to enter the service, but they will not be Witnesses any longer if they do. In order for a Jehovah's Witness to remain in good standing within the organization, he had better stay out of the service or any substitute for it. If he does accept work as a conscientious objector (or enter the service), it may bar him from ever becoming a part of the organization again officially.

They have lied to the Government from whom they get their exemption. They have deceived the officials to whom they give mock respect. They have dishonored the flag they refuse to salute. They have tried to appear in this *Memorandum* as part of the clergy whom they hate. They have tried to appear as part of religions they despise. Thus they "fight" for "freedom" to deceive the Government in order to avoid service obligations.

How do they get their new members to obey? From the start they criticize churches and the clergy. Then they tell these new converts that during a war, a person of one faith kills another person belonging to the same faith. They then show how Jehovah's Witnesses do not engage in war. Thus, Jehovah's Witnesses are the only peaceful people on earth.

Jehovah's Witnesses are not really ministers. The reader should be aware of that by now. They are at best salesmen of their heretic religion. If any of them claim to be ministers when at your door, ask them in what capacity do they serve in their "church"—not in the "ministerial fellowship" at the Kingdom Hall, but in their *own* church. Ask them when services are held. If you ask when they have *worship* services, it will be interesting indeed, for they have no worship services among themselves at any time. You will see he has no church, no pulpit, no following.

Ask any of these "ministers" if they are *allowed* to attend seminary, and see what they say. Ask if they study *systematic theology* under professional clerics. Ask the "minister" if they have taken or are taking courses in *homiletics* (composition and delivery of sermons) ; *hermeneutics* (the science of interpretation) ; *apologetics* (defense and proofs of Christianity) ; *eschatology* (study of future things) ; *soteriology* (the branch of theological science concerning salvation by Jesus Christ) ; *church history,* etc. You will quickly find out that they will not even know what you are talking about.

If they try to use a few Greek words, which is their favorite trick, ask them where they studied Greek and for how many years. Ask them what theological works they have studied or read and what commentaries they regularly refer to. If they try to give you a certain meaning for a word in Greek or Hebrew, ask them what lexicon or grammar they base their conclusion on. That will usually end the matter. By probing them thus you will see that they know little but what the Watchtower organization has put in their heads. There are a few exceptions, of course, but they are few and far between, and even *they* do not know much about what they are saying.

If they say these things you refer to are unnecessary and the Bible alone is sufficient, they are merely trying to escape from your difficult questions. Ask them why they need the Watchtower books they are using. Then try to find out why they use the unscholarly method of jumping from text to text and quoting these Scriptures out of context. Get them to read the Bible without doing so and they will begin to see that they are in gross error.

A Jehovah's Witness will wear a Government uniform if

it's the right kind. He can wear a mailman's uniform, for example, but not a military one. (However, this is only true if he became a mailman *before* becoming a J. W.!) During a war they will work in war plants and collect large salaries from steady jobs. They will manufacture the munitions and weapons, but they cannot take a substitute job for military service, like working in a hospital.

They are against holding political office, voting and serving on juries.

They will never aid in any charitable relief work, nor contribute to the Civilian Defense. They will not permit their children to salute the flag. Thus, their children grow up in an atmosphere of suspicion and hatred. They are taught that no authority is equal to that of *The Watchtower Society*. Thus, they despise church and pastor. They have a superior attitude about them, believing themselves to be better than others. Yet, they are generally the most useless citizens of any community.

What can one do about all this? What is worth doing? The concluding chapter will answer these questions.

Chapter Ten

WHAT TO DO ABOUT THE WATCHTOWER MONSTROSITY

T HAT THIS THING *The Watchtower* of the Russellites has spawned is a monstrosity, no honest observer can deny. As to the problem of what to do about it concerns us now.

If you are a Jehovah's Witness, you have two choices. You can remain in the organization in your lost condition and spend eternity in Hell. Or, you may seek Christ as your Saviour who will grant forgiveness for your sins and give you eternal life. While it is true that you may find salvation apart from any local church organization, you should seek the fellowship of Bible-believing Christians in a local church assembly, as a Christian must be identified with the visible Body, or Church of Christ. By faith in the redemptive work of the Lord Jesus Christ you become a member of God's universal family of called-out-ones. This is sometimes called the New Birth and precedes joining a local church of believers.

Your normal reaction to this invitation will be one of fear both of the organization and of individuals. Go to no one but the Lord in prayer. Read no other book but the Bible, for the time being. After you have been redeemed you will notice a change in your life; this change will affect your mind and body. You will have become a new creature in Christ (II Corinthians 5:17).

Do not fear that opportunities of service and work for the Lord will not be available to you. Your new opportunities will keep you busier than when you were a Jehovah's Witness. But that frustrating fear of being rejected will soon be gone, for you will have been born again, having passed from death unto life (John 5:24; I John 5:11-13).

You will then begin life anew as a child of God. This means you start out as a "babe." You will need time to grow in the Lord. Your entire way of thinking must be made over anew, and your outlook on life and everything else will be changed. As long as you remain yielded to the Lord, your every problem will be solved and He will carry your burdens. Your life will be one of a satisfied mind and a peaceful and contented heart. His grace will always prove to be sufficient for you.

Thus you will become really and truly acquainted with Jehovah the Father for the first time in your life, having come to Him through the Son. You will enter into an intimate relationship with Him—a personal relationship that you never thought possible in this life. You will feel His presence near you everywhere you go. Whenever you cry to Him in time of trouble, He will hear. He will be your constant comfort and ever guide you through life. Then, when this present life is over, He will take you Home to the dwelling-place of eternal glory to be with Him for ever and ever.

So fear not to come free, Jehovah's Witness. Your eternal Father waits with outstretched arms to welcome you. Fear no man, no matter how powerful he may seem to be to you. Shake off those shackles of bondage and slavery, and come free into the freedom of the children of God.

If you are a Christian and have an assurance of salvation, here is what you can do. When a Jehovah's Witness comes to your door and starts a sermon, wait until he gets to a passage of Scripture. Then bring your own Bible. Look up the text he is quoting. Read it within the context. Ask him why he is taking the verse out of its context. He will evade the issue and return to his sermon. When he comes to his next Scripture passage, read it within its context again. Then ask him why he is using *that* particular Scripture. He probably will not know why. By doing this you will draw him away from the Watchtower organization for a moment, and he will be an individual again, at least for the time being.

Feeling as a lonely individual facing the Bible and your questions, he will most likely leave at this point. He cannot think for himself. He is not allowed to, even if he is capable. He does not dare to speak as an individual apart from his organization. After he leaves pray that the Lord might honor the precious seed of His Word that you have sown. Never lose faith in what you have done. You have not given your own word, but God's Word. Have faith that it will not return void, and that God will save the one to whom you have just spoken.

This same Witness may return to see you. If so, tell him you have been praying for him, and ask him if he has found Christ as his Saviour yet. Be sure to give your own testimony of what Christ has done for you and what he means to you. Jesus Christ means nothing to him yet. He must be shown exactly who Christ is and what he himself must do in order to be saved. He starts out thinking he knows all the answers, but he will readily find out that he does not. Now use the following methods which will be briefly outlined.

If he says the soul dies and is therefore out of existence after the body dies, be careful how you argue the point with him. He will want to argue in order to confuse you. If he shows you Ezekiel 18:20, show him verses 21-28. Thus, the argument is answered by the Bible itself, right in the context. The reason Witnesses never read the context is that it usually shows up their misinterpretation.

Discovering that you are saved, he will quickly point out Philippians 2:12. Just as quickly you should point out verse 13. He never goes that far in his own reading, for he thinks he has made his point. He may try to prove to you that Jesus is inferior to the Father, in order to ridicule the Triune Godhead. He will show you John 14:28. Read on down to verse 31, where the Son gives commandment the same as the Father, showing equality. Again, the answer is in the context.

If you identify yourself before the Witness denominationally, you may miss the mark. He is always ready to argue against denominations, therefore, identify yourself as a Christian. Leave no room for an endless argument about some denomination. He will ask you what kind of a Christian you are. Tell him there is but one kind, found in many denominations and faiths.

He will then proceed to tell you what a real "Christian" is. He will end up by saying you must become a Jehovah's Witness. You simply cannot be a Christian according to his thinking because you are not in his organization. If he insists on good works as the means of salvation, read Romans 4:1-16. Insist that he read every word of it out loud. He will not want to because the Bible does not really mean much to him. If he will not read the Bible, refuse to talk further with him.

If a Jehovah's Witness accepts Christ as a result of your bringing the Gospel message to him, invite him into the fellowship of your church. But do not insist that he join, or get deeply involved in anything immediately. It takes a little time to grow in the Lord. Let him attend your church, or go to various churches if he so desires, until he feels at home among the Lord's people. He will feel strange in these new surroundings, and will need time to get adjusted. Sow no seed of hatred in his heart, cause no division to arise in his heart as to the proper church. Let the choice be his as much as possible.

Help him to begin to win others for Christ. If you are not very active in the work of the Lord, put him in fellowship with someone who is. Have him give his testimony in prayer meetings. In this manner he will grow accustomed to his new surroundings. If he was a public speaker in the organization, it will not be long before he will begin to preach and he will become an integral part of the church. Encourage him always to grow in stature spiritually and eventually come to full maturity as a man of God.

Always remember that his coming to Christ was not of your doing, but of God's. You were the instrument that God used to impart the Gospel. But the Holy Spirit will convict him of sin, and through Christ he will be saved and united with the Father. You are to sow the Word. Only God can save him.

It is in this manner that the heresy of Jehovah's Witnesses is being defeated today. In many churches there are converted Jehovah's Witnesses, sounding the warning against the heresy of *The Watchtower,* and in turn, always ready and available to lead another Jehovah's Witness to the Lord Jesus Christ. They need not put into operation a separate organization of their own, as they now have the *Holy* Spirit, who has replaced *The Watchtower* organizational spirit. Christ died to redeem the *Church,* and it alone is His "body." "The Spirit and the bride say, Come."

If you are NOT a Christian (a born-again one), there is little you can do to help a Jehovah's Witness. You must have salvation *yourself* before you can offer it to anyone else. The best thing for you to do is let the Jehovah's Witness go his way. Needless to say, he cannot help you. He will turn you farther away from the Saviour. If you become a part of his *Watchtower* organization, they will get you to turn others farther away from the Saviour.

If you are an official of a city, state or federal Government, and you have been wondering just what to think or do about these people, the best thing to do is let them alone. Not that they are of God, but they thrive on persecution. It pushes them deeper into their dark heresy. They believe they should be persecuted, and if you oblige, it makes them believe even more strongly than before that they are God's people. They have a persecution (martyrdom) complex.

However, they can be an obnoxious group at times. No government owes them anything, since they refuse to give allegiance to any government. Just remember that the smooth talk they give you is to deceive you and get you to do their bidding. They send their most eloquent men to persuade you to give them permission to do what they want. Judge accordingly. The Communists are given freedom to meet, and Jehovah's Witnesses have the same freedom on the same level.

Do not permit yourself to be impressed by their sincerity, zeal, energy and ability to speak fluently and eloquently. They are trained as organization men. It is their business to make such an appearance. They have a very highly inflated ego, and walk as if on clouds above everybody else. Let them know where you stand, and do not permit them to act as your overlord.

To the clergy, I say this: These people loathe, despise, detest and hate the Church and her Christ. They tell their people that laymen are dupes of a demonized clergy. Church people are told they have been tricked into believing almost anything they are told. Witnesses actively preach against the clergy from door to door every weekend. They say your church and all other churches are of the Devil. They endeavor to get people to leave the churches in order to fill their Kingdom Halls.

Pastors should warn their congregations against Watchtower heresy. They should be told what is in store if they listen to Jehovah's Witnesses. Pastors should tell their people to defend their church and their faith, using the Biblical methods outlined in this book. Jehovah's Witnesses are enemies of churches and the Lord Jesus.

This writer is not dedicated to writing against Jehovah's Witnesses. They are no more lost than anyone else who is unsaved. Yet it was thought that with a background of ten years in Watchtower activity some good might come of such a book, both to Christians and to those Jehovah's Witnesses who would be saved. To that end this book was written. It was prepared as a defense of the Christian faith as well as a proclamation of it, directed against the misnamed Jehovah's Witnesses. It does not pretend to be a profound theological work. Neither is it to substitute for the Holy Scriptures, as the Watchtower publications are for Jehovah's Witnesses.

It is at best, an aid to Christians and an exposé of Jehovah's Witnesses. When Saul of Tarsus was turned from unbelief to Christianity through the risen Christ, he immediately started to defend the faith he once fought against. So it is now with the writer of this book. The gospel became to him precious and worthy of defense against pernicious heresy. Many years were wasted in the darkness of Watchtower slavery, in activity designed to destroy churches and the effectiveness of the Gospel of Jesus Christ. Should any less work be done now that his soul has found the light of salvation?

Is free salvation a cause to cease all work? Or rather, should works not demonstrate the faith within (James 2:18)? The work of the Holy Spirit through Christians will never be done through laziness. Neither do sluggards work hard in the vineyard. The commission given by Christ to "make disciples of people of all nations" will not be accomplished by remaining silent.

Therefore it behooves us *all* who love the Lord to put forth a demonstration of faith by action (Ephesians 2:10). It is not for the purpose of impressing people, nor to try to impress the Lord. Neither is it to impress yourself with what you think you are accomplishing. But your love for Christ can be measured by what you openly demonstrate before others. Love can be shown. Very seldom does it remain hidden, unseen by others. Love knows no bounds. Love will drive you on when all else fails to move you.

So wake up, Christians! Wake up, pastors! Wake up, missionaries! Stop permitting Jehovah's Witnesses to spoil our reputation by pointing their accusing finger at us and the truth we hold.

Together then, we can walk triumphantly down the salvation road, calling to the lost and dying world, *Come with us!* Throw off your shackles and chains. Christ is ready to set you free!

Christians, what do you do when Jehovah's Witnesses hold a mass meeting in your town or city? Do you sit idly by while they canvass the entire area to spread their heresy? Do you meet force with force? Why not turn their convention into an opportunity to deliver the saving Gospel of the Lord Jesus Christ? For every leaflet that the Jehovah's Witnesses put in the hand of a passer-by do *you* offer a gospel tract to counteract it? Do you turn the tables on the Witnesses and hand out Christian material to them because you believe you have something more important to give them than they have to give to you?

Let Christians arise and meet the occasion. Greater is He that is in us than he that is in the world. Let us go forward in His power and strength and meet these folk with the message that leads to salvation. For every Jehovah's Witness let there be a Christian worker. For every *Watchtower* magazine let there be a Christian magazine. For every word of heresy spoken let there be a word of salvation. Meet this head-on, brethren, and see what God will do.

You do not need mass organization like Witnesses do. You will not need their organizational spirit, for YOU have the HOLY SPIRIT. Pray for the Lord to supply the printed material necessary, then to send the workers to give it out. Go out and meet Witnesses convened in your city, prepared with the Spirit and the Word. After you have given out the Word, pray together that there shall be reaping from what you have sown. As you work together, pray together.

Let us demonstrate what the power of God can do in and through Christians. God shall sustain you abundantly with His Spirit while you are thus engaged. When Jehovah's Witnesses are massed in your town and city, go forth and meet the Witnesses with the Bible and Gospel tracts. Show them you have risen to defend your faith. Through your ministerial fellowships, ministeriums or councils get others to join you, and bring as many from your church as will come. Never let Jehovah's Witnesses point you out in eternity and say, *"He kept quiet."*

Let us be on our knees together and we shall rise together. We are one in the Lord. Let us never become divided. Let us be as thoroughly *with* the Church below as we hope to be with the same Church *above*. Let us fight the good fight here and now. Let us never scorn the lost, but shed our tears in earnest prayer for them. Let us do unto them as someone once did unto us when we were lost in sin. May we ever be one in Him, now and forever. Amen.

> Faith of our Fathers! Living still
> In spite of dungeon, fire and sword,
> O how our hearts beat high with joy
> When'er we hear that glorious word!
> Faith of our fathers! holy faith!
> We will be true to thee till death!
> Faith of our fathers! We will love
> Both friend and foe in all our strife:
> And preach thee, too, as love knows how,
> By kindly words and virtuous life:
> Faith of our fathers! holy faith!
> We will be true to thee till death!